THE LIFE OF
JOHN J. HARDEN

PUBLIC MARKET

OUT FROM THE SHADOWS:

THE LIFE OF

JOHN J. HARDEN

BY BOB BURKE

Foreword by John E. Harden

KENNY A. FRANKS
SERIES EDITOR

GINI MOORE CAMPBELL
ASSOCIATE EDITOR

OKLAHOMA HERITAGE ASSOCIATION

Other books
by Bob Burke:

Lyle Boren: Rebel Congressman
3,500 Years of Burkes
These Be Thine Arms Forever
The Stories and Speeches of Lyle H. Boren
Corn, Cattle, and Moonshine:
    A History of Hochatown, Oklahoma
Like a Prairie Fire
Push Back the Darkness
The Irish Connection
Lyle H. Boren: The Eloquent Congressman
Dewey F. Bartlett: The Bartlett Legacy
Glen D. Johnson, Sr.: The Road to Washington
An American Jurist:
    The Life of Alfred P. Murrah
Mike Monroney: Oklahoma Liberal
Roscoe Dunjee: Champion of Civil Rights
From Oklahoma to Eternity:
    The Life of Wiley Post and the Winnie Mae

Printed in the United States of America
ISBN 1-885596-09-x
LC Number 98-67123
Designed by Carol Haralson

Oklahoma Heritage Association
201 Northwest Fourteenth Street
Oklahoma City, Oklahoma 73103
Oklahoma Heritage
Association Publications
Committee 1998

Facing page:
John J. Harden and Jane Harden, ca. 1928

FRENCH LICK SPRINGS HOTEL
WIGHT PHOTO

What if the glory of escutcheoned doors,

And buildings that a haughtier age designed,

The pacing to and fro on polished floors

Amid great chamber and long galleries, lined

With famous portraits of our ancestors;

What if those things the greatest of mankind

Consider most to magnify, or to bless,

But take our greatness with our bitterness?

W . B . Y E A T S

CONTENTS

FOREWORD

DURING THE MORE THAN THIRTY YEARS between my birth and my grandfather's death, I doubt that I spent more than three or four months in his presence, even though I was adopted by him when I was 12. "Daddyjack," as he was called by his children, was not one to sit down and read you the Sunday funny papers.

I remember that when I was a small child everyone in the Harden household was always coming or going somewhere. My grandmother was off to Bali, Aunt Jane to Switzerland, Aunt Frances to France, "Daddyjack" to Washington, and my mother and father off to a dude ranch in New Mexico. My brother and I stayed home with the servants.

After my return to Oklahoma City in 1976, I gradually became the repository for dozens of filing cabinets containing thousands of tightly-packed yellowed pages which were in effect a chronicle of the personal and business life of the grandfather I barely knew. Most of the protagonists and antagonists who are the subjects of this book are long gone, but much of Oklahoma's heritage is the result of the work and deeds of many of those mentioned herein. Few were saints and some were sinners, but most fell somewhere in between. I was constantly amazed at the multitude of long lasting friendships and loyalties developed by this man over the years.

Once in the early sixties, I attended a luncheon at the American Club in Buenos Aires. The guest of honor was Jim Farley, Postmaster General under Roosevelt. After the meal was over I went up to Mr. Farley and introduced myself. He immediately asked about the health of John J. and if all was well with the hotel in Acapulco. Pages of correspondence between John J. and Roy Howard indicate a great feeling of mutual admiration and fondness that withstood all the pressures of my grandfather's ongoing fight with the editor of the Scripps-Howard newspaper in Oklahoma City. These people and many others genuinely liked John J. for what he was as a person and not for what favors he might be able to do for them.

I had never known this side of "Daddyjack" and I don't believe that his children had either. From the files, it is apparent that he battled alcoholism all of his life. Over the years he entered many sanatoriums, including Meningers and John Brown's, trying to kick the habit. Drinking was the primary cause for an attempt at divorce in 1930 and a long separation from my grandmother which culminated in divorce in 1947.

A mutual nervousness existed between my grandfather and his children. They were all dependent upon his largesse for survival and he was prone to use this as a way of manipulating their lives. For a man with a yearly income of three to four million dollars it seems paradoxical that his letters sending two or three hundred dollars to his children would invariably end with the phrase, "treat it kindly, it was hard to come by." Many times on the same date his files would indicate that he was betting five or ten thousand dollars on the outcome of a football game or a prizefight. He would set his sons up in business and then withdraw his support if he disagreed with what they were doing. He and my grandmother blocked several opportunities for my Aunt Jane to marry on the pretext that the suitors were fortune hunters. Aunt Frances was somewhat of a Bohemian free spirit and was exiled from the United States in the 1940s, not returning to this country until my grandfather's death in 1962.

The business dealings, reflected in great detail in his files, show a picture of a man who understood political power and how to use it to his own benefit. He was probably the largest real estate developer in the history of Oklahoma. Quality and convenience were

John E. Harden as a baby, in Custer, South Dakota, where John J. sent John Hale and his family to manage a gold mine during the Depression in 1932.

his selling points and he always gave his customers their money's worth even though a portion of that worth may have been politically subsidized. John J. was a risk-taker who gambled and won more than he lost.

His political relationships on a local, state, and national level were strongly anchored in friendships built over a period of time. He was known as a man of his word who could be counted on to do what he promised.

As he grew older his health started to fail, the years of heavy drinking taking their toll. John J. was 60 years old when my father John Hale died. The youngest son, Jimmy, was 26 and somewhat of a playboy. It was about this time that John J. really lost interest in the continued growth of most of his business empire. His only real interest was the building of his hotel in Acapulco. Although it never prospered, it was for a period of four to five years the "in " place to go in Acapulco.

His final years were spent mostly confined to his bed in the home he built in Oklahoma City in 1927. He had direct lines to Las Vegas and most of the major race tracks throughout the United States. The executors of his estate had to battle the IRS once more over several hundred thousand dollas of winnings and losses. I think that "Daddyjack" might have smiled.

JOHN E. HARDEN
OKLAHOMA CITY, OKLAHOMA

THERE ARE ALWAYS SO MANY PEOPLE for me to thank when I have completed a book project. I love Oklahoma, its history, and its people. I am one of the few fortunate souls who is surrounded by helpers who share my excitement about Oklahoma.

Eric Dabney, my friend and legal assistant, always gets as involved as I do in researching the intricacies of some historical figure's past. This book is no different.

Debi Engles transcribed interviews and helped with computerization of the work.

I made a new friend during this project. John E. Harden, the grandson of John J. Harden, allowed me to spread papers and files in his conference room for six months while I laboriously plowed through a dozen or so file cabinets of his grandfather's correspondence and records. John E. often dropped whatever he was doing to guide me through the maze of paper. He and his brother David were gracious to provide their recollections and other valuable information in interviews.

Attorney Phil Daugherty and his brother U.S. District Judge Fred Daugherty were great sources of information on Harden's early years and the probate of his estate.

Carol Campbell, Robin Davison, and Mary Phillips at *The Daily Oklahoman* and Chester Cowen at the Oklahoma Historical Society made available photographs from their incredible collections.

I appreciate the Harden family research compiled by Cheryl Marie Battle O'Connor. Her information was the only available source of early Harden family history.

As always, Kitty Pittman, Carol Guilliams, and Melecia Caruthers at the Oklahoma Department of Libraries and Scott Dowell, Rodger Harris, Judith Michener, Bill Welge, and Fred Standley at the Oklahoma Historical Society pointed me in the right direction when I was stumped, looking for a source of needed information.

It was an honor to have Carol Haralson design the pages, photos, and cover of this book. She is truly an artist without peer.

It is an immeasurable joy to write books in consort with the Oklahoma Heritage Association. Executive Director Paul Lambert, Kenny Franks, and Gini Campbell not only give me great advice and counsel during each project but they are my good friends. They share my glee when I bounce into their office with some great revelation about the subject I am researching.

I owe a special debt of gratitude to my wife Chimene and my son Robert for never appearing to be bored when I insist upon reading my latest chapter to them. I am a lucky guy.

BOB BURKE

1998

IRISH ROOTS

The summer wind cooled the wrinkled brow of John Harden as he sadly stood with shoulders drooped at the graveside of his young wife. It was the early summer of 1849 in County Louth whose green pastures lay along the Irish Sea on Ireland's east coast. Mrs. Harden, like thousands of others, had died during Ireland's darkest hour, in the years of potato famine.

Potato blight, a fungus that literally consumed growing potatoes, devastated the Irish agricultural economy in the 1840's. Four years of horrible famine, labeled by historians as the Great Potato Famine, began in 1845. The smell of the rotting tubers in the fields hung over Ireland like a dark cloud.

By 1847 starvation and disease were rampant in Dublin, Ireland's major city. In the countryside, tenant farmer John Harden,

barely twenty years old, was trying to eke out a living raising pota-
toes and tending a few sheep. Typhus, famine fever, dysentery and
other deadly diseases went untreated because of a critical shortage
of medicine and doctors who valiantly tried to curb the mounting
tide of death and disease. Swarms of beggars, driven from their
homes by hunger or eviction, carried the seeds of fever wherever
they roamed. Government officials were overwhelmed as hospitals
were crowded to a point of suffocation. Patients were housed in
tents and "fever sheds" where they slept on bare ground.[1] In the
end Ireland was unprepared for the onslaught of epidemic that was
fueled by hunger and malnutrition. A Catholic priest who visited
his parish wrote:

> I beheld with sorrow one wide waste of putrefying vegetation.
> In many places the wretched people were seated on the fences
> of their decaying gardens, wringing their hands, and wailing
> bitterly the destruction that had left them foodless.[2]

John was in another world, remembering his beautiful Irish
wife. He was jolted back to reality when a small hand tugged at his
coat. John's heart rose to his throat as he realized he was now the
single parent of three small boys, Michael, James and John. He
turned and brought the children close to him and told them everything would be all right, even without their mother's comforting
touch.

Hard times continued in Ireland. John and his neighbors in the
parish of Cullen worked from daylight to dusk to break the hold
of famine on their land. They abandoned their back-breaking efforts in 1850 and followed a stream of almost two million immigrants to the "promised land" of America. Ireland lost one-fourth
of its eight million inhabitants during a ten-year span in the middle of the nineteenth century as a direct result of the death and
emigration caused by the Great Potato Famine.

John boarded up his meager thatched-roof cottage, packed a
few items of clothing and keepsakes, and headed for Dublin with
his neighbors Henry O'Neill, Andrew Cunningham, and Patrick
Rogers to book passage on a ship to America. The docks of Dublin

housed hundreds of expectant passengers. Men like John offered to join a ship's crew in exchange for passage.

The trip to the New World took nine weeks on a leaky sailboat. John kept a keen eye on his three growing boys. Playing in the salt air, the boys received their daily exercise on the upper deck of the boat as it rocked along through the choppy waters of the North Atlantic. Other families on board were not as fortunate as John and his trio. Lacking the money to pay passage for one of their children, one family smuggled him aboard as a stowaway. Another son died enroute to America and was buried at sea.

It was the beginning of a new chapter in the life of John Harden and his boys as they walked off the ship in New York City in the fall of 1850. John heard from other Irish immigrants about the rich farmland between the Genessee River and the Erie Canal in western New York. He worked odd jobs in New York City until he could save enough money to finance his trek westward.

John settled in Livingston County, in northwestern New York, where the agriculture-based economy depended upon the Erie Canal to transport crops to the population centers in central and eastern New York. The canal was completed in 1825 and stretched nearly 400 miles from Lake Erie, at Buffalo, to the Hudson River near Albany. Light boats maneuvered along the 40-foot-wide canal with the help of horses driven at a trot along the towpath. The waterway opened up for settlement the rolling hills of western New York and provided easier access for the many Americans who wanted to move farther west.

Soon John met Margaret Coragan, an Irish Catholic who immigrated from Ireland to New York with her family a few years before. They were married in 1851 and immediately added to the Harden clan. First came daughter Marian, followed by sons Luke, William, and Thomas, born in Fowlerville Township, in Livingston County, in 1858.

In 1866 John, Margaret and their seven children left their farm in western New York and moved to the other side of Lake Erie, to an Irish settlement in Ionia, Michigan. Ionia was the major town of Ionia County in central Michigan. John and his boys cleared timberland to make way for crops of corn, hay, and pota-toes. They soon moved to a larger plot of land near Hubbardston, a strong Irish Catholic community founded in 1849 by one John Cowman in the far northeast corner of Ionia County. The St. John the Baptist Catholic Church in Hubbardston became an impor-tant part of the Harden family life.

Thomas Harden was 20 years old when he fell in love with Mary Ann O'Connor in 1878. Their Irish lineage was almost identical. Both families had lived in the same County Louth in Ireland and had spent a short time in New York before settling in central Michigan. Thomas and Mary Ann were married at St. John the Baptist Catholic Church in Hubbardston November 7, 1878.

Thomas and Mary Ann had two children. John James Hard-en, born in Hubbardston October 13, 1884, was named after his grandfather. Daughter Marion Ann was born June 17, 1885. The Thomas Harden family unfortunately did not stay together long. Official records show Thomas lived with his brother in nearby Carson City, Michigan in 1894. Because of the separation, Mary Ann was listed in 1898 as a "widow" in the Lansing, Michigan City Directory. She lived with her daughter Marion. Thomas lived in Idaho for many years before moving to Santa Monica, Califor-nia where he died in 1937.

Mary Ann, still described as a "widow," and Marion had moved to another address in Lansing by 1900. Marion, at age 15, was identified as a music teacher. In 1906 Marion married South Bend, Indiana lawyer Vernon C. Hastings. She lived most of her life in Indiana prior to her death in 1960.

John James did not live with either of his parents in his teenage years. At age 16 he resided with his mother's sister Rose O'Connor McKenna and her husband Patrick J. McKenna who operated a dry goods store in Carson City. Delivering papers to earn money to help support his mother, John J. later described his years in Carson City as the happiest time of his life.

John J. Harden was an independent teenager. He worked hard at whatever task he was assigned. He made decent wages on his newspaper route and working odd jobs at his uncle's dry goods store. His circumstances in life forced him to depend on himself for his very existence. That training equipped him to later manage dozens of successful businesses and to amass one of the largest fortunes in Oklahoma history.

John J. graduated from high school in Lansing, Michigan in 1902 and was ready to take on the world.

Frances Hale Harden was nicknamed "Lulie" by grandson John E. Harden.
Courtesy John E. Harden.

A $25,000 STAKE

John J. Harden worked as a common laborer in a sugar cane processing plant in northeastern Nebraska in 1906. It was there he fell in love with 20-year-old Frances Fulsom Hale.

Frances was the beautiful and cultured daughter of the late David A. Hale, one of Nebraska's most influential political and business leaders of the last quarter of the 19th century. Hale served in the Nebraska State Senate and amassed a large fortune in cattle and real estate operations. He died in 1900 and bequeathed his fortune to his wife and three daughters.

Frances Hale was well-educated and brought up in the family mansion near Newman Grove, Madison County, Nebraska. A local newspaper called the Hale home, "a social center for the community."[3]

Frances still had $25,000 of her inheritance from her father when she married Harden in nearby Humphrey, Nebraska, January 2, 1907. Harden had always had big ideas of developing raw land into subdivisions in growing communities but never had enough money to cover land purchases and development costs. His new wife's dowry, and her willingness to invest in his dreams, was the stake that John J. Harden multiplied many times over.

Harden quit his sugar cane plant job and convinced Frances to move back to Ionia County, Michigan. They settled in the small town of Belding and immediately began buying land and subdividing it for residential homes. The Harden enterprise was a team effort. Frances' money financed the operation and she ran the office. Harden promoted the sale of lots. Their real estate venture was successful from the very beginning. Soon they moved to Grand Lake, Michigan and quickly sold out another subdivision.

David A. Hale, John J. Harden's father-in-law, was a powerful and influential voice in Nebraska politics in the late 19th century. Courtesy John E. Harden.

Frances gave birth to their first child, a daughter named Harriet Jane, on Valentine's Day 1908. As soon as mother and child were ready to travel the family moved south to El Reno, Oklahoma, using some of Frances' remaining inheritance to build a house on South Hoff Street. Harden had heard about the new state of Oklahoma and its growing population's need for housing.

The real estate market in El Reno in 1908 was wide open. On July 30, Harden formed the Harden Realty Company, an Oklahoma corporation whose original incorporators were Harden and L.A. Wilson and E.B. Cockrell, officers of the First National Bank of El Reno. Wilson and Cockrell had no financial interest in Harden Realty but were more than happy to lend their signatures to his incorporation effort. The bankers hoped Harden would borrow money from their institution and steer buyers of lots in his subdivision to First National for their installment loans.

From 1908 to 1911 Harden invested $24,000 and successfully developed the Lakeview Second Addition in El Reno and the College Addition in Vinita in northeastern Oklahoma. Hard economic times hit Canadian County in 1912 and lot sales dropped considerably. Harden eventually sold the remaining lots in the El Reno subdivision to H.K. Ricker in 1925 for $300.

From their base in El Reno Harden and his wife looked at other states for investment opportunities. Over the next several years they successfully completed subdivisions in Ohio and south Texas. Frances continued to keep the company's books while Harden traveled extensively overseeing the multi-state operation.

Harden and his family appear in the 1910 federal census in El Reno. The enumeration was completed in April. The household consisted of John J., Frances, Harriett Jane, a servant named Emma Robbins, and Harden's 53-year-old mother, Mary Ann, who had moved south from Michigan to Oklahoma to live with her son and his family.

Harriet Jane Harden, Frances and John J. Harden's firstborn, as a young woman. Courtesy of John E. Harden.

On November 7, 1910, Frances gave birth to their second child, John Hale Harden, in Birmingham, Alabama. No one knows why John Hale was born in Alabama. Harden had no known business connection with that state. However, the Hardens had developed a love affair with Florida and Cuba and one could speculate that John Hale was born early while the Hardens were on their way back to Oklahoma from one of their Florida excursions.

Less than two years later another daughter, Frances Ellen Harden, was born in El Reno October 15, 1912.

In 1915 Harden bought 40 acres along the Rio Grande River in Brownsville, Texas and developed a small subdivision. He reserved part of the land for a cemetery, Buena Vista Burial Park, a joint venture with Enrique Valentin. Harden, the consummate promoter, sold both building lots and cemetery lots to prospective buyers. The Brownsville experiment was no "bonanza" and Harden turned his attention to Oklahoma City.

In 1916 Harden began buying land "out in the country," on the northern fringes of Oklahoma City. The street car line was opening up the area between Oklahoma City and Britton for development and Harden wanted to be in on the ground floor. Another developer, G.A. Nichols, was buying up land north of 63rd Street, "way out in the country."

In 1917 the Hardens and their three small children moved into a house at 3405 North Classen Boulevard in Oklahoma City. Frances gave birth to twins March 27, 1918. Only one baby survived and was named James David Harden. James' birth certificate lists Harden's occupation as "real estate" and his mother's occupation as "wife and mother."

The timing of Harden's move to Oklahoma City was perfect. When World War I ended in November, 1918, 7,000 men who left the city for military service came home to find only 100 vacant living units.[4] The shortage of reasonably-priced housing offered a golden opportunity to men like Harden with subdivision development experience. Harden used money made in prior developments to buy every available parcel of land he could find in northwest and northeast areas of Oklahoma City. He talked with public officials and felt the pulse of the expanding community that jumped in population from 64,000 in 1910 to 91,000 in 1920. Harden was smart and correctly predicted in which direction Oklahoma City was growing.

The year 1919 was a peak of post-war prosperity for Oklahoma City. Citizens were optimistic about the future and passed a $1 million school bond issue by a six-to-one majority. Such optimism allowed Harden to borrow large sums of money to buy land for subdividing. He developed a close friendship, and later, a business relationship, with two banking brothers, Frank and Hugh Johnson, who believed in Harden and his ability to use borrowed money to make money.

Banking brothers Frank P. (left) and Hugh M. Johnson were business and social associates of John J. Harden and his family. The Johnsons provided much of the early capital used by Harden to build his empire. Courtesy Oklahoma Historical Society.

The Johnson brothers were natives of Mississippi and made a huge imprint on the banking industry in the early years of Oklahoma. In 1918 Hugh Johnson took over control of the State Exchange and the State National banks in Oklahoma City. Brother Frank was president of American National Bank. The banks merged, ultimately becoming the First National Bank and Trust Company of Oklahoma City in 1920, the largest bank, not only in Oklahoma, but in the Tenth District of the Federal Reserve System. The two Johnson families and the Harden family became very close and often traveled and vacationed together. Frances Harden included the wives of the Johnson brothers among her closest friends.

By 1920 John J. and Frances Harden had accumulated properties worth $6 million, equivalent to $56 million today, making them one of the richest families in Oklahoma as the Roaring Twenties began.

The chapel of Rose Hill Abbey in Oklahoma City was patterned after
King Tut's tomb. Courtesy John E. Harden.

THE CEMETERY BUSINESS

Harden made millions of dollars in the cemetery and mausoleum business from 1915 to his death. He was a master at taking raw land, landscaping it to perfection, and promoting the cemetery as the best in the area. Harden prophetically looked beyond the mere sale of cemetery lots and envisioned the construction of a mausoleum at every cemetery he owned or operated. The sale of crypts in a mausoleum proved to be an incredible source of revenue for Harden.

In 1916 Harden bought 153 acres in Evanston, Illinois. This Chicago North Shore area had a population of more than two million. Harden set up the Central Cemetery Company of Illinois with a perpetual charter to administer Memorial Park Cemetery. An irrevocable trust in the custody of the First National Bank of Chicago gave potential lot buyers confidence in Harden's venture. Over the next few years Harden built gardens, lakes, lagoons, greenhouses, and fountains to make the cemetery the most beautiful in Illinois.

Memorial Park was centrally located at Ridge Road and Harrison Street in Evanston. An advertising brochure described the cemetery as "befitting honor to the departed and a feeling to the family and friends in visiting, that they are yet near."

One of the keys to Harden's success in the cemetery business was his ability to surround himself with partners and business associates who not only shared his vision but were successful in their own right. The Memorial Park project in Illinois is a splendid example. Harden placed Robert G. McKay, a contractor in Wilmette, Illinois, in charge of the Memorial Park Cemetery. Other officers and members of the board of directors of the Central Cemetery Company were Sam D. Mangum, general manager of a large Chicago construction and paving company, and Roscoe D. Farmer, Harden's partner in at least a half-dozen projects in Oklahoma City in later years. Harden's associates were friends first, business partners second, a theme that helped make Harden a successful businessman.

Word of Harden's success in cemetery management in Texas and Illinois filtered back to Oklahoma. He was approached in 1917 by Ella Classen, the wife of Anton H. Classen, who planned to develop a small cemetery just north of the Belle Isle Lake in north Oklahoma City. Harden later bought a large piece of land that ran south from 63rd Street from Grand Boulevard west to Pennsylvania Avenue. The land south of Harden's tract, including the land where Penn Square Mall is now located, was owned by Anton Classen.

Harden's Memorial Park Mausoleum in Evanston, Illinois, was one of the finest edifices of its kind in the country. Courtesy John E. Harden.

Classen, an Illinois native who graduated with a law degree from the University of Michigan, came to Oklahoma City in 1897 as receiver and later registrar of the United States Land Office. He served several terms around the turn of the century as president of the Commercial Club, the predecessor of the Oklahoma City Chamber of Commerce. In 1902 he formed a real estate firm, the Classen Company.

Classen was one of the original owners of the Oklahoma Railway Company that operated Oklahoma City's street car system. In 1908 Oklahoma Railway Company built a power plant at Belle Isle Lake to generate electricity to run its street cars. Up to four million people a year traveled on

Ella Classen, wife of Oklahoma City pioneer Anton Classen, established a cemetery adjacent to Belle Isle Lake. She later sold the right to manage Rose Hill Burial Park to Harden. Courtesy *The Daily Oklahoman.*

its 38 miles of "interurban" tracks with 48 cars and 150 regular employees.[5]

Ella Classen and Harden struck a deal in the fall of 1917. Mrs. Classen would be paid 20 percent of revenues from the sale of lots and Harden could keep the remainder of any profit for his management of Rose Hill. Because it was illegal for an individual to own a cemetery in Oklahoma, Mrs. Classen deeded the 86 acres planned for the cemetery to a state-sanctioned property trust called the Rose Hill Burial Park. Frank W. Wycoff, J.E. O'Neil, and Charles W. Gunter were the original trustees who accepted the conveyance of the land in the trust document dated December 14, 1917. The trust, created by Mrs. Classen, was for a term of 999 years.

In addition to the 20 percent payable to Mrs. Classen, state law required Harden, as general manager of the cemetery operation, to place 10 percent of lot sale revenues into a perpetual fund account to assure that adequate funds were available for future maintenance of the cemetery.

Mrs. Classen's management contract with Harden was very specific, down to the minor details of landscaping, "[Harden] shall in accordance with modern landscaping architecture and gardening methods, adopted by leading cemeteries throughout the county, set out and nurture such plants, trees, shrubberies, deciduous or other flowers and vegetable decorations as may be reasonably required."[6] The contract also gave strong hints to Harden of what was expected of his management of Rose Hill, "[Harden] shall provide a suitable chapel or rest-house in and upon said grounds and an entrance gate…the same shall be suitable as a decent, modern, high grade, properly decorated, and first class burial park."[7]

Harden sold $52,000 worth of cemetery lot contracts at Rose Hill in 1919. But he learned from discussions with large cemetery owners in other states that the sale of crypts in a mausoleum provided the greatest potential for profit. The profit on lot sales was marginal because of the high cost of maintaining the land once it was subdivided into lots. On the other hand mausoleum space was sold on a pre-need basis for use in the future. The money collected was escrowed in interest-bearing accounts that would be used for construction of crypts as the need for burial space arose.

During 1919 Harden contracted with architect Sidney Lovell and builder Charles Lund to erect a small mausoleum at Rose Hill. Harden invested approximately $63,000 to build the Greek cross-shaped mausoleum known as the Rose Hill Community Mausoleum, on 3,452 square feet of land deeded to Harden personally by the cemetery trust.[8] Harden paid $863 for the small parcel of land and $21,000 for marble from the Georgia Marble Company. The mausoleum was an immediate success. By 1931, even in an economy driven downward by the Great Depression, receipts at Rose Hill topped the $63,000 mark, of which $45,000 came from the sale of mausoleum crypts.

Harden invested time and money into developing Rose Hill. Every view in the cemetery was like a picture. Harden created broad sweeping lawns, sunken gardens, and a beautiful lake. Rose Hill was convenient for the citizens of Oklahoma City, "just 10 minute drive from the heart of Oklahoma City."[9]

In the early 1930's Harden and Ella Classen had a disagreement over the amount of money she was to be paid from revenues of Rose Hill Burial Park. The controversy arose when Harden refused to pay Mrs. Classen a percentage of sales of crypts in the mausoleum he had financed. Mrs. Classen filed a lawsuit against Harden claiming 20 percent of all revenues earned by the cemetery operation, including sales in the mausoleum. The lawsuit was settled in January, 1934 with a new contractual arrangement that obligated Harden to deed to the Rose Hill Burial Park trust 51 acres of land that he owned adjacent to the cemetery and pay 10 percent of all revenues after that date to Mrs. Classen and her heirs. The additional land was needed for expansion of Oklahoma City's most popular cemetery.

By 1937 Harden had constructed a large abbey-type mausoleum facing Grand Boulevard on the east side of the cemetery property. Harden used his own funds to build the granite structure that a tastefully-done sales brochure called a "Westminister Abbey

In 1933, architect B. G. Noftsger presented Harden with this sketch of the mausoleum to be built at Rose Hill in Oklahoma City. Below, the completed Rose Hill Mausoleum, 1937. Harden took great pride in the completion of the mausoleum and the development of Oklahoma City's major cemetery. Courtesy John E. Harden.

for the people of Oklahoma." The inside of the modern mausoleum was constructed of Italian Carrerra marble with hand-painted ornamental ceilings, described in the brochure as "a place protected from the cold blasts of winter, the rain and the snow and from the hot sun in summer. A place where you may sit and meditate and be as far as possible alone with your departed loved ones."[10]

The crowning achievement of Rose Hill Abbey was its great chapel, patterned after King Tut's tomb, with marble and terrazzo floors and a pipe organ that rose majestically above the rostrum. Advertisements promised, "The music from its beautiful pipes will soothe and comfort as services proceed."[11]

Harden appealed not only to the emotional side of potential mausoleum customers who wanted peace and tranquillity for their loved ones, but also to the practical considerations of selecting a final resting place. The Rose Hill brochure emphasized security of investment:

> Provision for entombment in the Rose Hill Abbey is a good investment, a safe and permanent preparation for an emergency which all must certainly meet. What more fitting than to provide a resting place in the most beautiful surroundings possible where everything reflects life everlasting...Permit us to show you how to meet this problem in a dignified and convenient way, so that it need not be a financial burden. Meet it from your income in small installments.[12]

Rose Hill of Oklahoma City became one of the glittering jewels of the John J. Harden empire.

The year 1919 was extraordinarily busy for Harden and his cemetery businesses. He had bought 49 acres in Tulsa from Fred and Gunter Turner in 1915. Just four years later the Rose Hill Burial Park in Tulsa was open for business. Harden and his small band of salesmen sold $46,000 worth of cemetery lots. The cemetery property was deeded to the Rose Hill Burial Park Perpetual Care Fund, another property trust that Harden and his lawyers were well acquainted with. The original trustees were T.J. Harmen, Alva J. Niles, and C.A. Steele. Harden developed the raw land of Rose Hill Burial Park in Tulsa into one of the most beautiful and manicured cemeteries in Oklahoma.

Paul E. Forbes was hired by Harden as a caretaker at Rose Hill Burial Park in Oklahoma City in 1938. Forbes maintained the final resting places of many of Oklahoma's most famous citizens. Courtesy *The Daily Oklahoman.*

In 1925 Harden built a mausoleum at Rose Hill in Tulsa and sold out the space, more than $50,000 worth, in less than six years.

In 1920 Harden purchased 62 acres near Akron, Ohio and established Rose Hill Burial Park. Many cemeteries in America were named "Rose Hill" and Harden seemed fond of the name for his projects. In 1921 he formed Rose Hill Securities Company, a Delaware corporation, to pay the $56,000 for the cemetery land. Harden's partners in the Akron project were Oklahoma City bankers Hugh Johnson and J.W. Teter, respectively the president and vice president of First National Bank and Trust Company. In 1922 Harden placed funds from the sale of lots in a perpetual care fund administered by the Ohio State Bank and Trust Company of Akron. In 1923 lot sales rose above $17,000 with just $4,000 in expenses, leaving $13,000 to be deposited in the perpetual care fund for future maintenance.

Harden teamed up with Ponca City oil millionaire Lew Wentz in 1928 to purchase development property in Fort Worth, Texas. Together they created Rose Hill Burial Park, another cemetery that Harden owned until his death. Harden and Wentz each put up $100,000 for the land that was developed for a cemetery and a nearby housing addition.

Harden hired William Shelly Rogers and George R. Veeder to sell lots in the cemetery and promised them each one-fourth of the profits. It was a good deal for the salesmen. In 1929, the first full year of operation, lot sales were more than $130,000. The Depression was hard on the Fort Worth project. Sales dipped to $41,000 in 1931.

A decade later Wentz sold his 50 percent share of the cemetery to E.G. Seltzer, a veteran cemetery manager who worked for Harden in Oklahoma for several years.

Lee Harvey Oswald, the assassin of President John F. Kennedy, was buried in this Rose Hill Burial Park after he was killed by Jack Ruby in November, 1963.

NEW FORD FREE!

To Be Given Away At

Crestwood

Award will be made Saturday afternoon, December 11th, at 4:30 P. M., to the person submitting the best 50-word story or essay on Crestwood. Car is a brand new Ford sedan, fully equipped and now on display at Fred Jones Garage, 220 South Harvey.

Every contestant has an equal chance to win—and your story may be the lucky one!

There are no strings to this offer—all you have to do is visit Crestwood, register at the field office and enter your fifty-word story on the blank provided.

If your story is the best, you will win the valuable automobile absolutely free and without obligation of any kind. Only adults can register. And the writer must be present when the lucky name is announced.

Crestwood is a built-up neighborhood of delightful homes, with excellent schools, churches and amusement center near by and easy of access from the business district street car and automobile. Desirable restrictions assu the high character of the addition; and paved streets, stre lights, gas, water, electricity, and telephone service awa the home builder.

Yet with all of these advantages, desirable home sites Crestwood may be obtained for as low as $395.00, w down payment as low as $25.00 and with three years which to complete your payments.

But you must act quickly—for in this built-up neighb hood of hundreds of delightful homes, the desirable bui ing sites which are left at the low initial prices will not l long. See Crestwood today, and register for the valua free automobile!

REGISTER YOUR NAME TODAY!

By Automobile—Drive west on Sixteenth Street to Crestwood.
By Street Car—Take Las Vegas car to Nineteenth street, and walk three blocks west to Crestwood field office

YOU MAY WIN THIS CAR

John J. Harden Inc
711 Tradesmens Bank Bldg.   Maple 5848
OWNERS AND DEVELOPERS

City Office

Phone Maple 5848

Tradesmens Bank Bldg.

Crestwood Office

2558 West 19th Street

Phone 4-3781

HARDEN THE DEVELOPER

Through years of hard work, and by trial-and-error, Harden developed a sound formula for the successful promotion of real estate subdivisions. He well understood that prospective home buyers were interested in much more than just the appearance of a house and lot. The purchase of a home was often the largest investment a family would ever make. The modern homeowner was concerned about the location of the new addition, its distance from the center of the city, the condition of its streets and availability of utilities. An early Harden sales brochure answered the concerns of new homeowners:

> All improvements are now being installed—water, gas,
> paving, sewers, electricity and telephone lines. It is close to
> schools. Two city parks are located in the addition. All homes
> are restricted to brick, stucco or stone, assuring you of a high-
> class neighborhood. There will be no shacks or garage homes to
> depreciate the value of your investment.[13]

Harden used his powerful influence with public officials to gain favorable treatment in the installation of water and sewer lines in his subdivisions. His purchase of a paving company made his development of raw land into new additions even easier. Paved streets with sidewalks added class to an otherwise common housing development.

In August, 1924 Harden and Roscoe Farmer paid $55,000 for a barren "prairie" on the far northwestern outskirts of Oklahoma City, near present N.W. 23rd Street and May Avenue, and announced they would develop the subdivision formerly known as Jones Park Addition. Jones Park had lain undeveloped for a decade, because of the lack of modern improvements. Harden called his new development Crestwood.

Soon Harden's crews staked off lots, wide streets and a community park area. Within days the sounds of hammers and saws filled the vacant expanse of open land. Harden arranged with his bankers to begin two to three new houses a week for six months. Building materials were stockpiled so Harden's workers could complete one home and immediately begin another.

Harden planted 800 shade trees in the addition that was bounded on the south by Sixteenth Street and Villa Avenue on the east. It was Oklahoma City's largest real estate development to 1925 in what a newspaper called "the only tract of land within the city limits large enough to warrant a development project of the size planned by John J. Harden." [14]

When Crestwood was completely developed Harden had installed a mile and a half of paving, a mile of new sew-

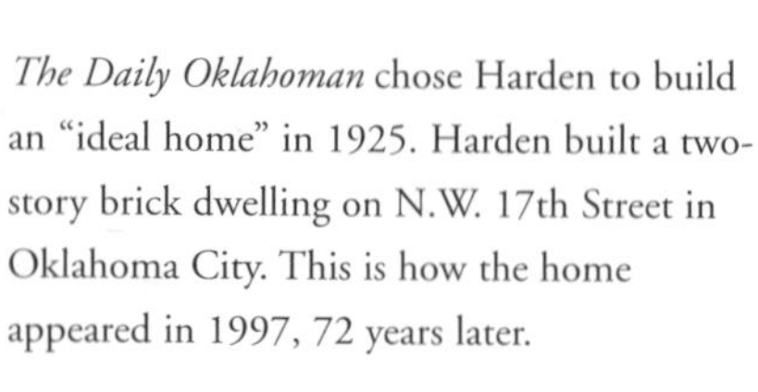

The Daily Oklahoman chose Harden to build an "ideal home" in 1925. Harden built a two-story brick dwelling on N.W. 17th Street in Oklahoma City. This is how the home appeared in 1997, 72 years later.

ers, a mile and a half of gas, electricity and telephone lines to serve the 700 building sites.

Oklahoma City's population had ballooned to an estimated 130,000 by 1924 and citizens were hungry for new homes. Crestwood was located on a hill, one of the highest points in Oklahoma City. It was a desirable place to live because of its easy access to the downtown business and industrial districts. Two street car lines, the Las Vegas and the Linwood, ran within two blocks of the addition.

Harden practiced his belief that homes could be sold quickly only if they were quality-built and reasonably-priced. The average completed home in Crestwood sold for $5,000. Homes ranged from a "5-room bungalow" on West 18th Street for $3,895 to a

"colonial two-story brick and frame six-room home" for $9,500. A down payment of only $500 reserved a home for an anxious buyer.

In less than four years most of the lots in Crestwood were sold. In *The Daily Oklahoman* R.G. Miller called Crestwood "one of the prettiest parts of the city."[15]

On November 21, 1924 Harden formed John J. Harden Inc., an Oklahoma corporation that took title to most of his development properties. The first officers of the corporation were Harden as president, Roscoe D. Farmer as vice president, and Charles H. Moureau as secretary-treasurer. The company had its main offices on the seventh floor of the Trademens National Bank Building.

One of the primary purposes of the formation of John J. Harden Inc. was to provide financing to new home buyers in Harden's developments such as Crestwood. Buyers signed a long-term installment agreement with ten percent down and the balance paid monthly at four to five percent annual interest. In 1932 John J. Harden Inc. was changed to Harden Mortgage Loan Company.

Harden hired his own building superintendent, F.T. Farra, his own architect, B.G. Noftsger, and dozens of foremen to boss crews that performed a variety of tasks from surveying land, to selling lots, to constructing houses. Harden was interested in building homes in his additions as well as selling lots to other individuals and builders.

Harden worked from sun up to sun down to keep his organization running smoothly. He encouraged his trusted lieutenants to make decisions and get things done "now!" Roscoe Farmer, Charles H. Moureau, Robert E. Lee "Bob" Finley, and George Simpson were among his most trusted cohorts. If any of them made a major business decision in Harden's absence, he ratified the decision when he came home. If Harden had tried to micromanage his vast enterprise, it would have most likely failed through bureaucratic entanglements and for lack of action.

Harden had a keen eye for spotting raw land fertile for development. On a trip through Ohio in 1924 Harden bought 133 acres for $40,000 in Columbus. The subdivision that rose out of the cornfield was called "North High Acres." Harden more than

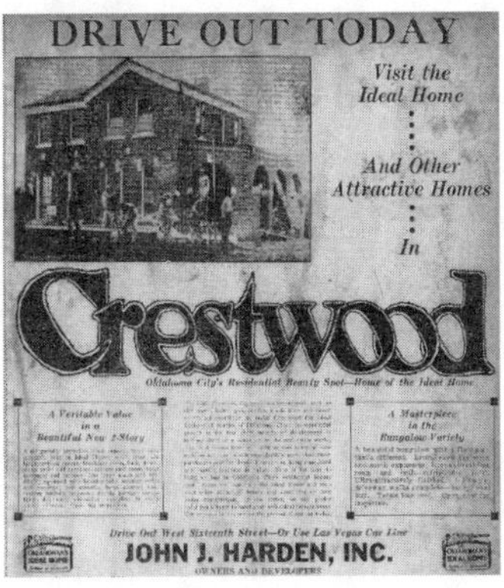

Harden purchased full-page ads in *The Daily Oklahoman* to publicicize his new development in northwest Oklahoma City in 1925. He was a master at marketing. He even gave away a new Ford sedan in a promotion in 1926 to lure potential home buyers to the Crestwood Addition. This photo and the photo page 36 courtesy *The Daily Oklahoman.*

doubled his investment in the Columbus development within five years. He possessed the knack for hitting growth areas such as Columbus, quickly making friends with the right politicians, and hiring the right people to develop, promote, and sell the land.

Harden's new additions in Oklahoma City provided opportunities for churches and businesses to expand and serve the owners of new houses being built. In 1925 Olivet Baptist Church bought five lots in Crestwood for $1,800 for construction of a new church facility. Other churches and small businesses purchased lots fronting on major streets that were set aside for commercial development. Realtors and individuals alike bought lots in Harden's new additions for speculation. The newspaper want ads were sprinkled with announcements that lots were for sale "by owner."

The Daily Oklahoman chose Harden to build its "ideal home" in 1925 in the Crestwood Addition at 2741 West Seventeenth Street between Randolph and Elizabeth avenues. The newspaper annually chose a project "whereby the prospective home owner and home builder may see the best in construction practice, gain ideas for his own home and see the many different essentials which enter into the planning and building of a house."[16]

The launching of the Ideal Home project on May 6 was a festive affair. Harden was joined by Oklahoma Governor Martin Trapp and Oklahoma City Mayor O.A. Cargill at a luncheon presided over by *Oklahoman* advertising manager H.E. Dreier at the Oklahoma Club. Trapp said one of his jobs as governor was to keep people satisfied and "when people are living in their own homes they are satisfied."[17] Mayor Cargill expressed his pleasure that new homes were being built so close to his home. Investment banker Thomas E. Braniff, who made the loan for the Ideal Home through his Braniff Investment Company, *Oklahoman* business manager Edgar T. Bell and Harden addressed the luncheon guests and told details of the project that was expected to be completed in 13 weeks.

Representatives of companies supplying products for the building and furnishing of the Ideal Home joined Governor Trapp, Mayor Cargill, and Harden at the groundbreaking ceremony. Mayor Cargill turned the first shovelful of dirt and posed for a picture with a host of public and business leaders that included Tom Braniff, W.T. Dimick of the Overhead Door Manufacturing Company, Edgar Bell, Wheeler Garrison and H.E. Dreier of the *Oklahoman,* F.P. Semple of Semple Manufacturing, W.M. Reeves of the Oklahoma City Tent and Awning Company, J.A. Maddox of Maddox Nursery, J.F. Harbour of Harbour-Longmire Furniture, and Walter Evans of Grand Paint and Paper Company. Harden's Crestwood sales force of George Veeder, G.E. Clark, J.D. Perry, and F.L. Pontius also appeared in the newspaper photograph.

Thomas L. Sorrey and Walter Vahlberg, architects who designed the student union building at the University of Oklahoma in Norman, planned and designed the Ideal Home. Harbour-Longmire Furniture furnished the interior. Weather strips were provided by Macklanburg-Duncan. The tile roof was supplied by Standard Roofing Company. Brick came from Acme Brick, the home was lighted by Oklahoma Gas and Electric Company, lumber came from Cullen Lumber Company and the Kelvinator refrigeration system was furnished by Semple Manufacturing.

The *Oklahoman* ran lengthy articles weekly on the construction progress of the Ideal Home. Veteran carpenter and foreman B.S. Moore was interviewed as forms were removed from the basement walls and framing began. Large photographs served as a pictorial essay on every phase of construction.

Harden capitalized on the free publicity of the Ideal Home. His sales of lots and new homes sky-rocketed. He ran full-page ads in the *Oklahoman* promoting Crestwood. One ad read:

> Away from the busy, dusty downtown streets—in a restricted neighborhood that is kept cool by nature's own electric fan—never a moment day or night that breezes cease to blow. Crestwood is conveniently located, too—just 2½ miles from Main and Robinson—and has electricity, water, sewers, gas, paved streets. . . 50 foot lots. . . 10 percent cash—balance easy.[18]

Governor Trapp and his wife were the first guests to inspect the Ideal Home when it was ready for public viewing on Sunday, September 6, 1925. Mrs. Dent Lackey sang several solos for entertainment as more than 500 people paraded through the home within the first hour. A newspaper account read like a Harden advertisement, "Favorable comment was heard on all sides both as to the convenience of the home and as to the simplicity of its furnishings. Perfect harmony in all the draperies and the furniture is to be seen in every room."[19]

Harden's publicity on Crestwood brought people from all over Oklahoma and from surrounding states to look at the "state's finest new houses."[20] In one week new homes in Crestwood were sold to James Mulkey of Ardmore, J. L. Henderson of St. Louis, D.G. Rixey of Indianapolis, and J.A. Menefee of Kansas City.

In November, 1925 Harden stepped up his promotion of Crestwood. Lot prices were reduced to $395 with "down payments as low as $25 and monthly payments as low as $15." Large display ads announced the December 11 giveaway of a brand new Ford sedan from Fred Jones Garage, 220 South Harvey, for the winner of an essay contest in which contestants submitted a 50-word story or essay on Crestwood.

Harden's overwhelming success in developing Crestwood was just an exciting beginning in an era of major growth for both John J. Harden and Oklahoma City.

An artist's conception of Harden's plan for developing
the Edgemere Park Addition in northwest Oklahoma
City. Courtesy John E. Harden.

Harden was one of the richest men in Oklahoma in 1925 and 1926. Everyone wanted to be Harden's friend. Even by mail casual acquaintances requested loans or invited Harden to participate in some off-the-wall investment scheme.

In 1925 Harden himself came up with a much-publicized development scheme involving the Oklahoma City Golf and Country Club. The golf course and clubhouse were located on 160 acres at Northwest 36th and Shartel. Harden wanted the land for a housing development so he offered an elaborate land-swap deal to members of the country club.

Harden owned 640 acres of land at Britton Road and North Western north of Oklahoma City. He proposed that the country club select the 160 acres most suitable for building a golf course in exchange for the land at Northwest 36th and Shartel. In addition Harden agreed to assume a $68,400 mortgage on the existing club property and pay $65,000 for the construction of a new clubhouse on the Britton Road property.

A special stockholders meeting was called to consider the proposal. Harden began "politicking" members of the country club of which he was an active member. Notes found in his files long after his death indicate that Harden thought such heavyweights as Tom Braniff, H.L. Berry, E.K. Gaylord, Harris Danner, John W. Shartel, G.A. Nichols, Pat Janeway, George Frederickson, and Roy Finerty agreed with him that the land swap was a good deal for the country club.

Country club president E.E. Westervelt, who had been instrumental in forming the country club in 1911, appointed a ten-man committee to investigate Harden's proposal. Members of the committee were Tom Braniff, E.M. Snedeker, P.A. Janeway, G.A. Nichols, E.A. Leibman, J.W. Upsher, George Frederickson, Henry Hoffman, O.P. Workman, and Roy Finerty.

Harden called on 77 members of the country club, 70 of whom said they would vote for such a proposal. But Westervelt entered the fray when a few members objected. In a few days the plan was dead as rumors circulated that the existing club land was actually worth $250,000 and that Harden wanted to bilk the club out of the valuable land.

Harden hired famous golf course designer James Dalgleish of Kansas City to survey his 640 acres on Britton Road to determine if the land was acceptable for the construction of a golf course. Dalgleish, who is credited with laying out golf courses from Missouri to Scotland, found Harden's land to be perfect for a golf course. He wrote, "I honestly consider your property as good or better than any other course I have either laid out or worked on."[21]

Harden penned a letter that was sent to each member of the

country club. He accepted as fact the allegation that he might make a lot of money on developing the 160 acres at the club's present location:

> I do not claim to be doing this in an unselfish way. If it succeeds, I will possibly make a great deal of money, but it is a big gamble and I might lose a great deal of money on it. If you don't believe it, look at the men in Oklahoma City today who have lost great sums of money in earlier days on just such kind of development. But I have a great deal of faith in Oklahoma City and I believe she has a very brilliant future, and I am willing to bet my money that she does go ahead.[22]

Stockholders turned down Harden's proposal in 1925 but Harden still wanted the property in 1930. By then country club members were ready to leave their old location and listened intently to several proposals. Harden offered to enter into a profit-sharing venture with club members. He estimated that the 160 acres, properly developed, could retail for a million dollars, providing a healthy profit for him and club members.

Oklahoma City realtor Harold F. Bradburn, representing a syndicate of local and outside investors, offered to pay $400,000 cash for the golf course land.

Realtor G.A. Nichols had built a new golf course for the Nichols Hills Country Club at North Pennsylvania and Grand Boulevard. He offered to trade his country club for the old country club, hoping the City of Oklahoma City would buy the old country club for use as a city park. Nichols proposed that a bond issue finance the acquisition of the property.

City officials liked the idea but never moved forward on pushing a bond issue to buy the property for use as a park. In the end club members voted for an even swap of their club for the new Nichols Hill Country Club.

By 1928 Harden had developed several major additions in Oklahoma City. These included Crestwood, Linwood Place, Meadowbrook, Edgewood, Edgemere, Harden's West 12th Street, and Young's Englewood. He also had built hundreds of houses and bought and sold hundreds of lots in the Linwood, Aurora, Classen North Highland, Summer Place, Grandview, and Lincoln Terrace additions.

Harden's success in subdivision development did not go unnoticed. Newspaper publisher E.K. Gaylord owned two lots in the Aurora Addition that he wanted to sell to Harden. Gaylord wrote, "Your new addition should move more rapidly than any real estate project in the last 15 years."[23]

One of Harden's biggest real estate successes occurred in 1928 with the major development of a new housing addition at Northeast 23rd and East Avenue, later Eastern Avenue and now Martin Luther King Jr. Avenue. The development was called Creston Hills. This was Harden's first development on the east side of Oklahoma City.

Ponca City oil man, newspaper owner, and philanthropist Lew Wentz joined forces with Harden to develop raw land in Texas and Oklahoma. Courtesy Oklahoma Historical Society.

Harden invited Ponca City oil man Lew Wentz to invest heavily in the Creston Hills project. The two millionaires agreed to split profits fifty-fifty.

Creston Hills was promoted as "the greatest real estate opportunity in Oklahoma City's history."[24] A prize of five bedrooms of furniture was given to the weekly winner of a contest to name a particular bungalow in the addition.

Seventy new homes were built by Harden in just three months after Creston Hills opened on October 1, 1928. By the end of the year Harden had sold 582 lots in all his additions for $459,000.

An historic event in December, 1928 boosted the incredible success of Creston Hills. Within three miles of the new addition an oil well spewed gas and oil from its belly for weeks, signaling the opening of the Oklahoma City field, the first time in America a significant oil discovery had been tapped within the city limits of a major city.

The opening of the Oklahoma City field created hundreds of jobs overnight. Workers needed houses so Harden and Wentz hired every available carpenter and brick mason in the area. As many as 60 houses were under construction in Creston Hills at one time.

The population of Oklahoma City increased by 10,000 in a period of a few months. Harden owned half of only 600 restricted residential building sites available in Oklahoma City in 1929. Even before the oil boom Harden's real estate empire controlled one-third of all the development lots sold north of the Rock Island Railroad tracks in 1928.

With prices and demand high, Harden and Wentz sold out Creston Hills in five months. Each man made a profit of $200,000, an enormous short-term profit in pre-Depression Oklahoma City.

Harden had a monopoly on the paving business in Oklahoma for many years. Here crews ready to complete work on a section of U.S. 66 east of Edmond in 1943. Courtesy *The Daily Oklahoman.*

WESTERN PAVING

An integral part of Harden's successful development of subdivisions was his ability to transform dusty and rocky streets into black and manicured avenues of asphalt. Harden purchased asphalt from Western Paving Company of Oklahoma City, a company that he bought in 1920 and built into one of the largest construction companies in the Southwest.

Western Paving was incorporated March 21, 1910 by Roscoe D. Farmer, later a full partner with Harden in many projects, and George A. Key who served as the first president of Western Paving. Shortly after its incorporation Farmer became the major stockholder of the company that paved roads with rock asphalt mined from deposits near the southern Oklahoma town of Dougherty in Murray County.

Rock asphalt was a naturally occurring mixture that resulted from oil seeping into limestone and sandstone deposits millions of years ago. When the lighter oil drained away, the heavier crude impregnated the limestone and sandstone, thus creating rock asphalt.

Since nature made the mixture, rock asphalt could be used to surface streets and parking lots with a minimum of effort. It could be laid "cold" after mixing it with sand and gravel. Man-made asphalt, a blend of heavy crude, sand, and gravel had to be heated in a costly asphalt plant and laid hot to get the best result. Scientists of the time felt rock asphalt was superior to the artificial mix because of its ingredients being naturally impregnated with crude.[25]

Major deposits of rock asphalt were found in only six states: Oklahoma, Texas, Alabama, California, Kentucky, and Utah. Murray County was the only county in Oklahoma where any sizable deposit of the mineral was ever found. Geologists surmise that the rock asphalt was exposed to the surface in Murray County because of the unique geological formations that were created when the earth buckled in ancient times in the Arbuckle Mountains region.

The Dougherty pit, located on 960 acres along Rock Creek about three and a half miles from the Dougherty station on the Gulf, Colorado, and Santa Fe Railroad, was discovered around 1895. As many as 600 men were employed on a sporadic basis to mine the asphalt. The land was originally allotted to the Chickasaw Indians and the tribe received royalties on sales of rock asphalt from the beginning of commercial production.

Several attempts were made from 1910 to 1920 to commercially produce and market the rock asphalt. Continental Asphalt Company and Foursome Producing and Refining Company both failed in their efforts to make money from the project. Asphalt was hauled over primitive roads from the pit to the railroad station at Dougherty, originally called Strawberry Flat, until a four-mile spur was built in 1917. Continental Asphalt built a community house with 42 rooms to provide housing for workers. Historian Opal Hartsell Brown described the house in her history of Murray County, "A huge balcony circle the high walls of the lobby, and there was a beautiful fireplace below. Sometimes as many as 15 familes lived in this modern structure, where entertainments and dancing was held."[26]

In 1920 Harden bought an interest in Western Paving from Farmer who had purchased control of the corporation from nine smaller shareholders. Harden and Farmer continued as equal shareholders in Western Paving for most of the decade. Later Harden became president of the company, bought out Farmer's share, and transferred Western Paving's assets to Harden Mortgage Loan Company.

With Harden as its president Western Paving created a near monopoly in the paving business in Oklahoma City and the entire state in the 1920's. Harden's friendship with politicians and his superlative business acumen allowed him to procure paving contracts from Oklahoma City to Clinton to Duncan. All over the state

Harden's rock asphalt mines near Dougherty in southern Oklahoma were surrounded by mine shacks and service buildings of all sorts. Courtesy *The Daily Oklahoman.*

Western Paving trucks dumped loads of cold rock asphalt on primitive streets and roads. Western Paving paved thousands of miles of city streets and state highways.

The numbers taken from the tax returns of Western Paving are unbelievable for a business in Oklahoma in the Roaring Twenties. In 1922 the company received $1.7 million dollars in paving contracts. In 1924 receipts were $1.5 million dollars.

Roscoe Farmer ran the day-to-day operations of Western Paving. M.L. Curry joined the company in 1925 as field superintendent of the paving operation. Three decades later Curry owned one of the largest construction companies in the state.

The paving business became so lucrative by 1922 that Harden formed two more corporations, Harjo Gravel Company, and Central Material and Supply Company, to develop gravel pits for use in the asphalt operations. Farmer was listed on tax returns as the general manager of Central Material and Supply which employed 40 men and sold $200,000 worth of gravel in 1922.

From 1920 to 1923 Western Paving bought rock asphalt from Continental Asphalt at Dougherty. When Continental went into receivership in 1923, Harden and Western Paving leased the Dougherty rock asphalt pits, updated the asphalt crushing plant, and hired hundreds of miners to work the pits.

Harden made big-time money from his paving business. One money-maker was his direct contracting with cities and towns, county commissioners, and the Oklahoma Highway Commission to pave public roads. Often Western Paving was not the low bidder, especially when concrete construction of roads and highways became popular.

To counter heavy criticism from his opponents Harden began a publicity campaign to convince public officials that asphalt re-

In addition to rock asphalt, Harden's companies mined thousands of tons of gravel from the pits around Dougherty in Murray County. At its peak, Harden's asphalt mining operation employed 1,000 workers. Courtesy Oklahoma Historical Society.

quired far less maintenance than concrete. Newspaper ads proclaimed that a stretch of 23rd Street in Oklahoma City paved by Western Paving had required only $5 in maintenance in five years. Harden argued that as newer cars could be driven faster, the smoothness of asphalt was far more desirable than the "klippety-klop" sounds created while driving across the joints between sections of concrete.[27]

Early in his business career Harden learned how to use paving bonds to finance paving projects both in his subdivisions and on public streets in other additions. In 1923 the Oklahoma legislature was encouraged by Harden and many public officials, including Governor Jack Walton, to pass legislation authorizing "paving districts." House Bill 189 was signed into law by Walton in March, 1923.

The bill allowed any group of landowners, no matter how small, to petition the governing body of a city or town for paving of its streets. Owners of more than 50 percent of the land adjacent to the street had to approve the petition. Once approved by the governing body, bonds were issued to pay for the project. The bonds, plus interest, were retired by assessing each landowner his pro-rata share of the total cost of the project. The assessment became a lien on the property and was paid out in annual installments.

Cities and towns were required to issue bonds within 30 days after the paving district was legally approved and notice of its establishment was published. The contract for paving was to be awarded to the "best bidder," not necessarily the "lowest bidder."

The paving district legislation resulted in a flood of petitions from homeowners who wanted to improve the value of their homes by having paved streets. Harden made money two ways out of the paving district scheme. He earned profit from his company laying the asphalt and from drawing interest on the paving bonds he or one of his corporations bought. At one time during the peak of paving activity in Oklahoma City, Harden and his companies owned almost a million dollars in paving bonds. He eventually had to sell some of the bonds at 60 cents on the dollar during the Great Depression to keep up his cash flow.

Harden drummed up his own paving contracts by hiring men to circulate petitions for paving districts all over Oklahoma City. In 1928 Phil Daugherty was a brand new lawyer in the Franklin Petroleum Building in downtown Oklahoma City. He officed next door to two of Harden's hired petition circulators, one of whom was named Bill Bradshaw. Daugherty and his younger brother

Fred, who worked for his brother as a typist for a nickel a page, struck up a friendship with Harden's men who worked out of an office "with no name on the door."[28] Fred Daughtery later became a general in the Oklahoma National Guard and was appointed U.S. District Judge for the Western District of Oklahoma by President John F. Kennedy in 1961.

Harden spent $20 million dollars on water, sewer, gas, and electric line improvements to his subdivisions in the 1920's, improvements that were then given over to the City of Oklahoma City and private landowners. Even though he made gigantic personal gains from laying millions of dollars worth of asphalt on Oklahoma City streets, Harden was proud of his contribution to the betterment of life for his neighbors. Corn fields and wheat fields became sparkling subdivisions in a growing community. There were times during the decade when Harden and his various enterprises provided 1,000 jobs with a payroll of over a million dollars a year, one of the largest payrolls in Oklahoma.

Harden's cash flow from his real estate development and paving operations was tremendous. He made even more money from playing the stock market. While vacationing at the Pancoast Hotel in Miami Beach, Florida in December, 1925, Harden wired buy and sell orders to his attorney Charles Moureau in Oklahoma City. In the week before Christmas Harden bought more than $300,000 worth of stock in such companies as U.S. Steel, United Cigars, General Electric, Hudson Motors, Postum, and Chrysler Corporation.[29]

The 1920's were good to John J. Harden.

Placards printed by Harden to announce his new hotel were distributed to restaurants and truck stops within 10 miles of Hobbs. A postcard hailed the establishment as an oasis, a beautiful 110-room fireproof hotel amid the Southwest's largest oil field. Courtesy John E. Harden.

EXPANSION OUTSIDE OKLAHOMA

As early as 1920 Harden was looking for business opportunities anywhere there was money to be made. He joined with Oklahoma City bankers Hugh Johnson and J.W. Teter in the purchase of a 25-acre oil lease with seven pumping wells in the Burkburnett Field in Wichita County, Texas. Harden had to borrow half of the $375,000 he paid for the producing lease, a lot of money in 1920 in the speculative oil business.

At first the oil lease appeared to be a major bonanza, producing 4,000 barrels a month for three months in a row in late 1920. Harden worked a deal with Aetna Petroleum Company to lease the partnership's interest for a cash payment of $50,000 plus $25,000 a month. If the oil would have continued to flow, Harden, Johnson and Teter would have made a small fortune in a few years. However production declined drastically through 1921 when Aetna forfeited the lease. Harden and his fellow investors were happy to sell the lease for $40,000 in December, 1921. Harden never again was tempted to invest heavily in the oil and gas business even though he often had large sums of cash available for investment.

Harden had dabbled in business interests in other states since he settled in Oklahoma in 1908. However, with America's economy booming in 1926 he stepped up his efforts to make money elsewhere. Cash flow from his Crestwood development in Okla-

homa City made the bottom line of his financial statement even stronger than before. It became easier and easier to borrow money and line up partners for investment opportunities.

Harden targeted for development several hundred acres of pasture land northeast of Amarillo, Texas in the spring of 1926. He and his family had spent most of the winter vacationing in Cuba and his entrepreneurial spirit was at work, even while laying on the beach. His dreams of a new city with a model city park, a large theater, and an eight-story hotel near Amarillo were big. He needed partners.

Harden found 259 acres "within walking distance of downtown Amarillo." It was actually 24 blocks. Harden, John W. Coyle

of Oklahoma City, and J. Ben Russell announced their intentions to develop a new addition on the property and formed the Ridgemere Development Company. The investment agreement was handwritten on stationery from the Hotel Palo Duro in Amarillo until lawyers could draft necessary documents. Coyle and Russell put in $10,000 each for 20 percent of the profits. Harden kept 60 percent of the company which immediately began developing the land as Ridgemere.

The Hotel Harden (left) in Hobbs was the center of activity in eastern New Mexico. Its coffee shop was a popular meeting place for would-be oil barons involved in the development of oil fields near Hobbs. Courtesy John E. Harden.

Harden financed his Amarillo projects at the First National Bank of Amarillo. His financial strength was communicated to the Texas bank in letters from Ben Mills, executive vice president of Liberty National Bank of Oklahoma City and J.W. Teter, vice president of First National Bank of Oklahoma City. Teter wrote, "Mr. Harden is a capable businessman and, knowing him as we do, we do not believe he would enter into an agreement he did not see his way clear to carry forward."[30]

Ridgemere lots were sold for the low price of $200 to $400. Harden's ads in Amarillo newspapers were strikingly similar to the ads that enabled Harden to sell Crestwood in Oklahoma City so quickly. Lot sales began June 18 with easy terms, $50 cash and $15 a month. A typical newspaper ad gave instructions to prospective buyers:

> Under the card giving "description" will be a red card with the word "sold" on it. When you detach the description card this will show to others that these lots have been sold. ARE YOU FARSIGHTED? Buy one of these lots for your son or daughter. After you get them paid for, let them grow in value for one or two years and see what a handsome nest egg you will have. It will send them through college, or give him a start in business and you will never miss the money.[31]

Harden patterned his development in Amarillo after Crestwood in Oklahoma City. The streets were paved with asphalt. Water, sewer, gas, and electric lines were installed so homebuilders could begin construction on the 50 ft. x 150 ft. lots immediately.

On August 1, 1926 Harden's lawyers created yet another corporation, the East-Amarillo Development Company, which immediately purchased almost 1,000 acres a half-mile east of the Ridgemere Addition on the Panhandle Highway. Harden launched a brand-new suburban city called East-Amarillo. The area was a developer's dream. Plans were announced by Amarillo city fathers in late August that a $500,000 cotton mill, a $15 million dollar power plant and a $400,000 natural gas pipeline would be built within three miles of the land Harden had bought.

Harden sunk thousands of dollars into advertising his new project, East-Amarillo, which opened on September 4. He rented booth space at the Tri-State Fair in Amarillo and held drawings for free lots in the new addition. Full-page newspaper ads announced the development as "A City in Itself—on Panhandle Highway." [32]

George Veeder was named general manager of East-Amarillo. A plat of the planned city was published in local newspapers and showed land reserved for a city hall, churches, playgrounds, and a community center.

East-Amarillo was an astounding success. Harden joined Veeder and a dozen salesmen in a newly-constructed administration building at the front of the development. In the first month of operation 247 lots were sold for more than $112,000. House construction began immediately.[33]

Overnight get-rich stories fueled lot sales at East-Amarillo. It was reported that one E.G. Langley paid $65 down on a $595 lot, held it one month, and sold the lot for $1,200, an amazing $605 profit on a $65 investment.[34] When other Texans read the story Veeder and Harden were covered up with new customers. Newspaper ads proclaimed, "Double and Treble your money on building sites in East-Amarillo."[35]

When the project was two months old, lot sales had reached 411, for a total of $213,000. In November Harden left his sales force busily writing contracts and returned to other projects in Oklahoma and Fort Worth, Texas.

By 1928 Harden was already partners with Ponca City oil man Lew Wentz in the Rose Hill Burial Park in Fort Worth when Harden spied a $200,000 piece of property just two blocks from the campus of Texas Christian University and 15 minutes from downtown Fort Worth.

Harden proposed that he and Wentz go fifty-fifty on the development of a new addition to be called Bluebonnet Hills. Wentz was in Los Angeles when he received Harden's offer. On May 26 he wired Harden who was resting for a few days at a hotel in Mineral Wells, Texas, and Wentz said he wanted in the deal and would put up half of the $200,000 necessary to buy the land. Wentz actually ended up paying the entire $200,000 because Harden borrowed his $100,000 from Wentz.

Bluebonnet Hills sported the usual pluses of a Harden development—paved streets, city sewers and water, gas, electricity and telephones. Long, graceful, sweeping curves replaced old fashioned square corners on the streets of the addition.

Harden sent George Veeder from Amarillo to Fort Worth to manage the project that began selling like hotcakes to Tarrant County residents. Harden and Wentz split $60,000 in profits on first-year sales of $110,000.

After the stock market crash in 1929, Bluebonnet Hills failed to fulfill Harden's predictions that he and Wentz could each make $200,000. By 1931 they were suffering huge losses and Wentz questioned Harden's handling of the investment. Harden went to Fort Worth and cut expenses of the operation, including the salaries of the salesmen, "It is my belief that every one can live cheaper this year than they did last, and the business they are doing there does not warrant any more than what I am giving them."[36]

By 1932 Wentz and Harden closed the books on the development and sold the remaining lots at a loss.

Harden often fished and hunted in New Mexico and loved the dry climate. He was convinced that Hobbs, New Mexico would become the oil headquarters of the Southwest after oil was discovered nearby in 1929.

In 1930 Harden built a three-story modern, fireproof hotel and dozens of small homes in a development known as New Hobbs. Pauline Jarrott was placed in charge of the 110-room hotel which opened November 22, 1930. Harden hosted a giant party to celebrate the opening of the hotel. Friends and business associates came from as far away as New York City for the gala event.

The Hotel Harden offered steam heat, hot and cold running water, and telephone service in each room. Most of the rooms had a private bath and rented for a very reasonable $1.50 per night. The hotel was owned by Lea-Mex Development Company, another legal corporation in Harden's financial maze. Harden and his trusted allies, George Simpson and Roscoe Farmer, were the three incorporators of the New Mexico corporation.

The coffee shop at the Hotel Harden became the "in" place for Hobbs residents. A local newspaperman reported, "Their meals are suggestive of home cooking and their daily luncheon specials are both delightful and economical. You find no rigid formalities or stilted magnificence in practice at the Harden but a rare air of hospitality pervades the entire atmosphere."[37]

The Hobbs project almost cost Harden his life. He was flying from Oklahoma City to Hobbs in his new tri-motor airplane to inaugurate the new hotel. During the flight, the plane lost power, forcing the pilot to crash land in the New Mexico desert. Harden and the pilot were shaken up but suffered only minor scrapes and bruises. Harden sold the tri-motor immediately and never flew again.[38]

The Hotel Harden and the surrounding development became vitally important to Harden as a large source of revenue during the Great Depression. When profits from projects in Oklahoma and elsewhere were slim, Harden's investment in Hobbs paid the bills.

In 1928 Harden's opponents pulled no punches. The first cartoon shows Harden standing behind the stage curtain while Oklahoma City Mayor Walter Dean announces a new program. A later cartoon accuses Harden of being paid by city officials in paving contracts. Courtesy *The Daily Oklahoman*.

HARDEN VS. MAGEE

arl C. Magee made his living attacking politicians and other public figures on the front pages of newspapers. He had been educated in his native Iowa as a school teacher but turned his interest to the practice of law shortly after he arrived in Oklahoma in 1903. After a few years in the Sooner State Magee moved to New Mexico and found himself in the newspaper business as a reporter for the *Albuquerque Morning Journal* by 1920.

Magee, a practicing Methodist and Mason, attacked "practically every person of any prominence in both political parties of New Mexico," during his seven years as a scribe in that state. When he left New Mexico a rival editor called him a "bull in a china shop who broke up an awful lot of fine ware while smashing the stuff that needed to be eliminated." The *Santa Fe New Mexican* accused Magee of having no purpose in life but to keep himself in the spotlight and to keep good men out of public life for fear of his attacks. The paper concluded, "As a 'reformer' in New Mexico he was done, busted, exploded, punctured."[40]

While in New Mexico in 1925 Magee accidentally shot an innocent bystander during a hotel lobby altercation between Magee and former Judge Davis L. Leahy.

From his post as editor of the *Oklahoma News*, Magee blasted Harden's business and political practices. Courtesy *The Daily Oklahoman.*

The shooting was the climax to a long and bitter political feud that had begun when Judge Leahy sentenced Magee to prison after he was convicted of criminal libel for the publication of editorials attacking a former New Mexico Supreme Court justice. Magee was sentenced to prison twice by Judge Leahy but was pardoned both times by the governor of New Mexico. Magee was charged with manslaughter but was acquitted by a jury.[41]

Magee was hired in 1927 as the editor of the *Oklahoma News,* an Oklahoma City daily newspaper owned by Scripps-Howard, one of the nation's largest and most influential newspaper chains. The *News* began publication October 1, 1906 as a one-cent newspaper, one of more than 50 newspapers and periodicals published in Oklahoma City before statehood. The *News* outlasted the great majority of those newspapers, and for 33 years was the only major competition for *The Daily Oklahoman* owned by E.K. Gaylord.[42]

John J. Harden was introduced to Magee by a mutual friend, A.R. Hubenstreet, owner of the New Mexico Construction Company. Hubenstreet wrote Harden and described Magee as a "staunch and valuable" friend who was "practical" and would not be mislead by "political intrigues which would tend to put you in a most embarrassing position."[43]

Harden used the Hubenstreet letter to strike up a friendship with Magee who promptly used his editorial pen to support Harden in a city-wide bond issue vote in the fall of 1927. Harden credited Magee with "lining up the labor vote" and convincing voters to approve bonds for new streets and sewers.[44]

The honeymoon between Magee and Harden was short-lived. In November, 1927, Magee began a personal attack upon Harden that is unequaled in the annals of Oklahoma reporting. For a seven-month period in late 1927 and in 1928 Magee filled his column "Turning On The Light" with allegations of corruption and wrongdoing against Harden. The following is but a sample of Magee's statements about John J. Harden:

> Harden is a Catholic and a very wet wet. . . He is a
> king. . . Harden is rapidly becoming the unelected and
> unofficial, but actual manager of Oklahoma, and everybody in

it...This pickle-peddler has a capacity to manage. . . He managed himself into wealth through the evasive ownership of cemeteries...(Harden) is an enemy of the state, engaged in exploitation through the highway department and uses political methods which no decent man can countenance. . . [45]

Only weeks after Magee took over as editor of the *News,* he blatantly accused Harden of manipulating the adjournment of the state legislature that was meeting in special session "with its eyes on the possible impeachment of Governor (Henry) Johnston and Fred P. Branson of the supreme court."[46] Magee alleged that Harden and two other major paving contractors, C.S. Beekman and Harry Kannady, and Judge James R. Armstrong "moved heaven and earth" to help the governor adjourn the legislature. "They framed and executed the deal that led state senators suddenly to flip flop and adjourn the session," Magee wrote.[47] Magee accused Harden and the other alleged conspirators, whom he called the "Big Four," of conspiring to buy-off state senators to adjourn the legislative inquiry of the governor. Magee listed specific amounts Harden had allegedly used to bribe certain senators in counties where county commissioners were urged to build asphalt rather than concrete roads. Harden was cited as the owner of the only rock asphalt mines in the state and therefore must have "picked up the reins and managed its [the legislature's] adjournment."[48]

The State Highway Commission was convinced by Harden and other contractors that asphalt was the best material for road construction in Oklahoma. When the Commission suggested that Canadian County officials change their request for matching funds from concrete to asphalt surfacing, Magee cried foul and called Harden the "brains" behind the scheme. He erroneously told his readers that asphalt cost $8,000 a mile more than concrete and that the Big Four had lapped up $400,000 in contracts from the highway commission. Magee complained that the state administration was controlled by men who have private axes to grind, "the governor appears to be helpless. The highway commission reflects his attitude. So we are blown up. And, the public pays the freight."[49]

Harden wrote the newspaper, the "first written statement I ever made to a newspaper."[50] He pointed out that his rock asphalt operation had sold only 16 percent of its production the previous year to the state highway department. The profit of $6,000 on those sales, Harden said, "hardly justifies an implication for shifty dealing that your paper implies."[51] Harden denied having any close relationship with members of the State Highway Commission, "I personally have met only one member. . . and that was a casual introduction by a mutual friend in the lobby of a local hotel." Harden also denied contributing even a penny to the legislative controversy, "We are running this business in a high-class way and we expect to sell rock asphalt on its merit to counties, towns, and to the state, no matter who the governor is."[52]

Magee opined that Harden and Governor Johnston were now in bed together, "a klan-dry governor and a Catholic-wet contractor suddenly found very much in common."[53] Magee was open in his labeling of Governor Johnston as a Klansman.

Mr. Carl C. McGee,
c/o Oklahoma News,
C i t y .

Dear Carl:

          I had a fine letter from Mr. A. R. Hubenstreet and he certainly went the full limit in recommending you as a real friend and square shooter. I am inclosing you a copy of my letter to him.

          You certainly hit this town at the right time, because I am very frank to say that if you hadn't arrived, the Oklahoma News would have made the terrific mistake of at least being against a portion of the bonds voted, and I believe that no small amount of the credit for the great success is due to both your writing, and the speeches which you made, supporting the bonds. I think the biggest thing you did in this connection was lining up the labor vote, because they certainly had their heads set to go against all issues.

          With best personal regards, I am,

                    Yours sincerely,

Relations between Harden and Carl Magee were cordial at first.
Courtesy John E. Harden.

Magee sporadically curtailed his attacks on Harden to actually brag on the developer. Magee admitted that Harden's development of many subdivisions had probably helped Oklahoma City. He even admitted that Harden had made much legitimate money out of the building business.

Harden's close friendship with Roy Howard, Chairman of the Board of the Scripps-Howard newspapers, made the battle between Harden and Magee even more intriguing. Harden and Howard had become hunting and fishing companions years before nad their two families often vacationed and traveled together.

Howard had taken over Scripps-Howard in 1925 after working his way up the ladder of the newspaper business since the turn of the century. He was one of a half-dozen of the most influential newspaper executives in America.

At first Harden did not discuss with Howard his battle with Magee and the *Oklahoma News*. But as Magee turned up the heat, Harden wrote Howard in mid-January of 1928. The letter began with, "I have hesitated to write because I have the fear you will think I am trying to tell you how to run your business."[54] Harden detailed Magee's allegations that Harden had bribed 23 state senators with $100,000 in cash and paid former Judge Charles B. Stuart $10,000 cash to defend the Governor. Harden told Howard that he had never met Judge Stuart. Harden said he had "written this letter several times, each time tearing it up."[55] "I would be a damn poor friend of yours if I did not give you this information, and I think we are both big enough to regard this as a business incident and that it has nothing to do with our personal relations which are ace high, in my book."

Somehow, the vicious fight between Magee and Harden did no permanent damage to the close friendship between Harden and Howard. When Howard received the January letter from Harden, he immediately sent a telegram assuring Harden that nothing in the incident would have the "slightest bearing on our personal relationship."

From the very beginning Howard refused to intervene with Magee, believing that that the man was "100 percent honest."

"He'll be wrong in his facts at times. . . No one of us is infallible, but if I am any judge of him, he'll be the first and the most willing to admit his error."[58] Howard reaffirmed his friendship with Harden, "I see no reason why I should have to sacrifice my great respect for Magee because of my personal friendship for you. Inversely, I see no reason why I should have to sacrifice my personal liking for you because of my great respect for Magee."[59] Howard closed the letter by trying to explain his loyalty to his editor:

> You are enough of a Mick to understand and value loyalty.
> It's the binding force of great businesses and great successes but,
> to be effective, it must be bilateral. I want Magee's loyalty. I
> know that I can't have it unless I am loyal to him.[60]

Harden fought back with a powerful weapon, his pocketbook. He withdrew his large advertising budget from the *News.* When the public market was opened, Harden answered the advertising solicitors from the *News* with "not a damned cent." Harden wrote a letter to *The Daily Oklahoman* about the effectiveness of that newspaper's advertising, a direct attack upon the *News* and its editorial policy. Magee editorialized, "Mr. Harden thought $45,000 would force Scripps-Howard to yield to his demands for protection. It didn't. It will not."[61]

Throughout the newspaper battle with Magee, Harden was encouraged by his friend Howard to sue Magee if "he is wrong or has in any way or to any extent damaged you in your community." And that is exactly what happened. On July 12, 1928, shortly after Harden returned from the Democratic National Convention in Houston, Harden's attorneys J.S. Ross and H.C. Thurman filed in the district court in Oklahoma County a $250,000 libel suit against Magee and the *Oklahoma News.*

The lawsuit charged that Magee published a series of "craftily planned editorials. . . attacking and criticizing Harden, and directing toward him suspicion and abuse. . . and falsely holding the plaintiff. . . to be a person guilty of the crime of bribery and corruption. . . all of which have exposed the plaintiff to public hatred, contempt, ridicule and obloquy, and have tended to deprive him of public confidence, and have injured him in his occupation."[63]

Harden released to the press what he called "my first and last public statement on this case."[64] Harden said his investigation had revealed that New Mexico was glad to get rid of Magee. Harden blasted Magee for attacking many public officials such as Judge C.B. Ames and U.S. District Judge Edgar Vaught and for belittling Harden's development of the Oklahoma City public market, "which I believe is one of the outstanding civic developments of the last few years."[65] Harden ended his tirade, "Since coming here he [Magee] has not stood for one constructive thing. . . he hates everybody except himself."[66]

A defiant and confident Magee responded to the lawsuit by devoting his entire column to the subject the next morning. He predicted that Harden "may live to see the day when his colleagues will be cussing him for the mess he has got them all into," and said he felt belittled by the fact that he had been sued for only $250,000 "in this modern day of one million dollar libel suits."[67]

The Magee-Harden fight gained much notoriety in Oklahoma in the late 1920's. One reader of the *Oklahoma News,* a Bernice Smith of Oklahoma City, said the fight sounded like "two women fighting on a Monday morning over the back fence." Mrs. Smith suggested Magee and Harden "get out and fight it out like men and quit raging in the papers."[68] *The Capitol Hill Beacon* called Magee "the singer of hymns of hate," and reprinted a Santa Fe newspaper editorial gleefully announcing Magee's departure from New Mexico. One of Oklahoma City's leading Baptist ministers, Charles Henson, defended Harden, the Catholic, and called Magee the "arch character assassin." Rev. Henson applauded Harden's contributions to the growth of the city and said his heart often burned within him when he read the tirades of Magee. Henson urged Harden to take a stand in his lawsuit, "Your character will shine all the brighter after having been assailed by the slimy pen of Carl Magee."[69]

JOHN J. HARDEN, Inc.

BUILDERS AND DEVELOPERS
REAL ESTATE

Oklahoma City

TELEPHONES:
CITY OFFICE M-5848
CRESTWOOD OFFICE 4-3781

OFFICES:

SUITE 205-212 PETROLEUM BUILDING

January 14, 1928-

Mr. Roy Howard,
250 Park Avenue,
New York, N. Y.

Dear Roy:-

I have hesitated to write you in regard to this matter, because I have the fear that you will think I am trying to tell you how to run your business, but I believe that you have a very serious situation here, and one that should have attention.

It looks to me like Carl has got the News in a serious jam by accusing twenty-three of the State Senators of receiving $100,000.00 in bribes for the calling off of the Special Session. These Senators are, of course, very angry. It looks like the News might have twenty-three libel suits filed in twenty-three different counties of the State, or wherever the newspaper is sold. This would make you a lot of expense and trouble even if they did not collect one cent of damage. My analysis of the situation is, he went a little too strong; if he had listened to Beak Parker and myself at our noon luncheon when you were here, he could have stayed on the fence on this proposition, given both sides hell and come out of it in fine shape, but in following his own judgment, after only about five weeks residence in the State, he took the damnedest licking that I ever saw a newspaper man take. After taking this licking he became vicious and wanted to punish somebody. In one article, he stated that I paid Judge Stuart the sum of $10,000.00 to defend the Governor. I went to Stuart's office yesterday upon a telephone call from him, and Major Cruce, (your attorney) had to introduce me to him. This was an absolute lie, probably given to him by some political parasite about town, however, I have no personal animosity toward him for this, because it was not serious and I rather considered it good advertising, because my side won the fight. His next move was to accuse the Senators of selling out for $100,000.00; naming the exact amounts some had received, but not mentioning any names. My information on this from your attorneys, is that it is a serious acquisition to make.

A few days after he wrote the article about me, I met Pete Hamilton, and in a kidding way said, "I thought I would sue the News, simply to get Carl into court to prove the source of his information." A little later, Pete advised me that he wrote you, Deak and Tom Sidlow, saying that I was going to sue the News and, of course, you know that it don't make a dam bit of difference what this fellow tries to do to me, I am not going to start a Law suit with my friends.

I would advise that Deak Parker get Major Cruce on the telephone and check up the information that I am giving you.   It is certainly too bad, because Carl made a wonderful start here, was getting over in a big way, and my personal opinion is, that he has knocked everything in the head.

I have written this letter several times in the past week, each time tearing it up, fearing as I said before that you would think that I was trying to run this newspaper and God knows if Carl had taken advice from me, instead of from the political parasites and panhandlers that I know he did take it from, this whole situation could have been avoided. Carl made the serious mistake of figuring that everything was chaos here, he wanted to destroy the Government and Supreme Court and regardless of what he thought of the personnel of the Supreme Court, it was still a Supreme Court.   The reason the Legislature did not convene was because they were up against the Law, and were fundamentally wrong.   I happen to know how the decision was arrived at to adjourn, and this reason was that the prominent lawyers of the Senate had to admit that they must stand for Law and order.

You will realize that I have been in a serious position, I did not want to take a hand in this, but it has gone to a point where I think that I would be a dam poor friend of yours if I did not give you this information, and I think we are both big enough to regard this as a business incident and that it has nothing to do with our personal relations which are ace high, in my book.

I am sending a copy of this letter to Deak and Tom Sidlow; for the reason that Pete advised them that I was going to sue the News, and I dont want them to think that this could be possible.

I will be in New York within the next two weeks, and of course, we will get together.

I don't believe this letter calls for an answer, but knowing that your idea of running newspapers is that your editors must have reliable information and knowing that Carl has gotten himself out on a limb on absolute misinformation, I felt it my duty to give you these facts.

With best Wishes to Peg and yourself, I am,

Yours sincerely,

JJH/H

Harden kept Roy Howard fully briefed on his battle with Magee.
Courtesy John E. Harden.

The *Tulsa Daily World* saved some of its most stinging comments for Magee. The newspaper said Magee "wields a wicked machine and when he throws his typewriter he usually breaks a rib or two."[70] In a quarter-page scathing satire, the *World* opined that Magee was terribly egotistical and always had to be the center of attention:

> Unless he [Magee] is allowed to be the whole show, he kicks over the water can, accuses the clown of wearing makeup, eats the peanuts and boldly proclaims he never fully trusted a single member of the troupe. . . When God said, "Let there be light," it was Magee who turned on the gas and struck the match. If you don't believe us, ask Magee. . . Such men as Magee would be dangerous if given power. They do not lead others but are led by others; the moment they discover they are not leading they fly the track and chase the shadow in an effort to destroy the substance.[71]

Magee actually apologized for an incorrect story that he wrote in the summer of 1928 about Harden backing Oklahoma City Chamber of Commerce official R.A. Singletary in a state senate contest in Oklahoma County. Singletary was pitted against incumbent Senator W.C. Fidler who was backed by the *Oklahoma News.* Magee ridiculed Singletary as the puppet of a paving contractor and incorrectly wrote that Singletary and Harden were in business together. Singletary lashed out at Magee and called him a "dirty liar" and charged that Magee had once killed a man in New Mexico and then alibied his way out of trouble. Magee admitted killing a man but said it was justifiable. When the facts about Harden's lack of involvement with Singletary were laid on his desk, Magee backtracked.[72]

Magee went to great lengths to criticize Harden. When Magee launched his campaign to unseat Supreme Court Justice Fred P. Branson, Magee wrote one of his more light-hearted editorials:

February 3, 1928-

Mr. Roy W. Howard,
250 Park Avenue,
New York City, N. Y.

Dear Roy:-

        I had a talk with Carl yesterday.   All of this time,
of course, I thought he was indirectly shooting at me on this
$100,000.00 business;   I find that I was entirely mistaken. Carl
also finds that the information on the $10,000.00 fee which I was
supposed to give Judge Stuart to defend the Governor was wrong.
On the basis of us breaking fifty/fifty on misunderstandings we then
proceeded to have a two hours conversation and we ironed out our
own differences and I hope we will not have any more.   We then talked a little about Pete Hamilton and we agreed that I should have a
short talk with Pete.   I proceeded to do this today without in any
way indicating any ideas which you had.   I simply talked to Pete
on the basis that an organization pulling apart certainly could not
succeed, whether it was a newspaper organization or a real estate
organization similar to mine.   Pete quite agreed with me that
the thing for he and Carl to do were to work hand in hand for the
big success of the News and I believe this is going to happen.

        With my personal matters ironed out with the News, I am
now going to turn the general managership of said News back to you,
Deak and Bill Hawkins, and while you boys have not had much experience
and are so very unsuccessful in the newspaper business, I am of the
opinion you know a little more about it than I do.

        I certainly made not mistake in getting to Oklahoma City
Tuesday morning, because different things had developed to a point
where it would have been dangerous to have stayed any longer.

        With Best Regards to Peg, Deak, Bill and yourself, I am,

                                Yours sincerely,

JJH:H

ROY W. HOWARD
CHAIRMAN OF THE BOARD
250 PARK AVENUE
NEW YORK

May 7, 1928.

<u>PERSONAL</u>

My dear John:

I have two letters from you -- one undated, received several
days ago, and another, dated May 3rd, which I received
this morning. The first one was that containing the cut-
tings from Carl Magee's column. As regards the May 3rd
letter, will say that I am mighty sorry indeed that I
missed seeing you in New York. My office states, absolutely and unqualifiedly, that they received no call from
you and I am forced to believe that you may have gotten
one of the telephone numbers from the book which represented our foreign advertising offices, or one of the other offices, rather than my own up-town office at 250 Park Avenue,
the number of which is Vanderbilt 3075.

I was expecting you and rather kept things open in order to
have a chat and, consequently, was a bit surprised when I
did not hear from you.

Now, as to the first letter. I must be perfectly candid with
you, John -- and I am certain that I can be without in any
way interrupting or damaging our friendship.

Inasmuch as I cannot and will not debate Carl Magee's worth and
ability with Pete Hamilton, who is Carl's own business associate, I cannot debate it with an outsider.

I believe that Carl Magee is 100% honest. I believe him to be
one of the most effective and certainly one of the highest
type representatives of American journalism. I have no
quarrel with you or with any other man who disagrees with
me in that judgment. However, out of my very great fondness for you and because of my similar belief in <u>your</u> hones-
ty, I want to offer this suggestion which you are at perfect
liberty to discard if you see fit. Don't make the mistake
of believing that Magee is either ineffective or insincere.
Don't make the mistake of believing that Magee would harass
you merely for the sake of proving that he has no fear of me
or for the sake of demonstrating his independence. Carl
Magee understands his independence -- his right to independent editorial thinking, writing, and action -- more clearly
than you understand it. I am certain that I am not flatter-
ing his intelligence when I say that so long as he is on the
job in Oklahoma, or any other Scripps-Howard paper, he is

Roy Howard tried to stay out of the Harden-Magee war of words. Courtesy John E. Harden.

not only at liberty to but is expected to exercise the same
independence and the same freedom of action that he would
exercise were he the controlling stockholder of the paper.
I may be wrong but I don't believe that the thought that I
would ever seek to warp his judgment on an editorial matter
or seek to make it conform to my own, ever entered his head,
at least not at any time since he has been in the organization long enough to understand our methods and to realize
our own appreciation of his intelligence and his integrity.

I don't ask you to like Magee. I don't believe that I would even
go so far as to say that I think it possible that your minds
will ever meet but I hope, if you entertain any such thoughts,
you will be able to disabuse your mind of the idea that
Magee is either foolish, untruthful, or ineffective. He'll
be wrong in his facts at times -- of course. No one of us
is infallible but, if I am any judge of him and his technique,
and I think I am, he'll be the first and the most willing to
admit his error once the proof of that error is made clear to
him.

Boiled down, the situation is simply this. I have no desire to be
put in the position of urging you to like Magee. Inversely,
I do not want you to be in the position of seeking to make
me dislike him. When I want to go fishing or hunting, I'd
rather go with you. When I want to play the newspaper game,
I'd rather play it with Magee. I see no reason in the world
for mixing the two up. I see no reason why I should have to
sacrifice my great respect for Magee because of my personal
friendship for you. Inversely, I see no reason why I should
have to sacrifice my personal liking for you because of my
great respect for Magee.

Hence this note.

You are enough of a Mick to understand and value loyalty. Its the
binding force of great businesses and great successes but, to
be effective, it must be bi-lateral. I want Magee's loyalty.
I know that I can't have it unless I am loyal to him. Consequently, my Stephen Decatur-like attitude toward Magee.

I'm very much interested in your report of the house in Houston.
Here's hoping the plumbing is okey and that the Frigidaire
works.

                              Cordially yours,

John J. Harden, Esq.,
205 Petroleum Bldg.,
Oklahoma City,
Oklahoma.

RWH:WEV

JOHN J. HARDEN, INC.

BUILDERS AND DEVELOPERS
REAL ESTATE

Oklahoma City

TELEPHONES:
CITY OFFICE M-5848
CRESTWOOD OFFICE 4-3781

205-12
PETROLEUM BLDG.

November 16, 1928-

Mr. Roy W. Howard,
250 Park Avenue,
New York, N. Y.

Dear Roy:-

     I am enclosing you a clipping which Carl had in today's paper. I have red penciled the portion in which he states that I said, "I am through with politics, unless there is some business in it for me." This is another damn lie, and probably one that was told him by some curbstone politician.

     Now Roy, I have done everything that I can possibly do to protect myself from libelous statements from Magee; I sued him some four months ago, and he has been stalling the case as long as he possibly can in the courts, this as you know, can be done for a certain period of time, without my being able to force it. I have no way to defend myself against Magee, he has a newspaper and I have'nt, and I have arrived at this conclusion, I believe, that I am entitled to a square deal from you, and if our friendship is the kind that I will not give you a square deal, and that you will not give me a square deal, then I don't want that kind of friendship.

     As to the rest of the article for your information, and this is information that Magee could easily acquire, at least seventy-five percent of the paving done by the Western Paving Company in the past two years has been done on my own property and assessed against my own property. On this, we have paid the City, an emgineering fee of eight per cent, or something over $100,000.00 a year. I estimate that this engineering cost the City about twenty-five thousand dollars, so the City has made a profit of probably $75,000 a year from my operations. His contention in this article, is that paving petitions should be allowed to accumulate until there is about 100,000 yards ready for a letting; this would take a year to accomplish and in the meantime no property could be developed, and the City would be standing still. You don't realize that we are doing more business and more to build Oklahoma City, than all of the rest of the real estate men combined. I do not claim to be doing this for philanthropic purposes, but even at that, all of us like to put big things over and we don't always look at the dollar profit that is at the other end of the line. I believe you made a sensible business deal in Denver, and I do not think there was anything unethical about it, but I want you to understand that, since I have been doing business in Oklahoma City, I have not performed one act that was any more unethical than your deal in Denver. I would like to have an expression from you in regard to this.

     With best personal regards, I am,

              Yours sincerely,

JJH:H

We haven't any beans for our bean-shooter, but we can buy
them from John Harden, bean merchant. Branson has already
assured us that he isn't John Harden. So Branson will get none
of our money, even if Harden does. We are so desperately in
earnest in our determination to hurt Branson with our bean-
shooter that we would buy beans from John Harden to do the
job. My, how mad we must be at Branson![73]

Magee's editorials and a host of other political problems spelled
defeat for Branson at the hands of Republican lawyer Thomas G.
Andrews in the District Seven Supreme Court race in eastern Oklahoma.

Harden's lawsuit against Magee and the *Oklahoma News*
dragged on for five years. When Magee resigned as editor of the
newspaper in 1933, Harden dismissed the case. He wrote Roy
Howard that the new managers of the paper were "good hustlers"
and he, Harden, intended to give them back some of his advertising business. Howard answered Harden, "I was glad to hear that
the obsequies had been said over the law suit which seemed to
cause so much worry to our mutual friends while you and I were
off on a hunting expedition together." [75]

The *Oklahoma News* published a daily paper only another half-
dozen years and shut down its presses for good in 1939.

Carl Magee is remembered in Oklahoma history for an idea totally unrelated to the newspaper business. Magee's solution to the
parking problem in front of businesses in downtown Oklahoma
City was a device that drivers could deposit money into and park
for a short period of time. Magee's idea was perfected by re-
searchers at Oklahoma A. & M. in Stillwater. The world's first
parking meter was later installed in downtown Oklahoma City.

Following pages: Roy Howard's wonderfully diplomatic attempt to spare his
friendship with Harden, while standing firmly by his journalistic principles.
Courtesy John E. Harden.

SCRIPPS-HOWARD NEWSPAPERS

W. HOWARD
AN OF THE BOARD
PARK AVENUE
NEW YORK

November 20, 1928

Personal

My dear John:

I am enclosing copy of a letter which I am today addressing to
 Magee. I think it speaks for itself.

As to the paragraph which I deleted, I can only repeat what I
 have previously said. I have no intention of permitting myself to be drawn into any controversy between you and Magee.

I have explained to you our system of operation. That system
 has been in effect for fifty years. I couldn't change it
 if I would and I wouldn't change it if I could. It is the
 keystone of our arch. You're a business man and you have
 a sense of proportion. You know that nothing could possibly
 be more absurd than for me to attempt to interject my persona
 ideas or my personal desires into the handling of issues
 which are purely local for any one of our papers.

In these local affairs it is impossible for me to know all of
 the governing facts. It is impossible for me to even know
 the local atmosphere of the situation. Further than that,
 I am no superman. There is certainly no reason to believe
 that my judgment on a purely local issue should be better
 than that of the editor on the job. In every instance the
 editor is staking everything he has -- his reputation as an
 editor and his financial interests--on the conduct of his
 paper. My interest in every instance is but a fractional
 one.

Quite aside from all this, and whether you either understand it
 or accept it as a fact, an editor's job is of necessity an
 impersonal one. Many great journalists, men of the type of
 E. W. Scripps, Lord Northcliffe, Paz of La Prenza, Buenos
 Aires, and to a certain extent F. G. Bonfils of Denver, have
 deliberately cut themselves off from social contacts, avoided
 clubs, churches and lodge entanglements, in order to further
 stress the impersonal nature of their work.

I have never felt disposed to go this far, in fact, have never
 felt it necessary to do so. Up to now I have been able to
 maintain my social contacts and retain my friendships without
 compromising my singleness of purpose as an editor.

As I have many times told you and as I am sure you know intuitively, I have a very real affection and regard for you as a friend. I believe that to a degree at least my affection for you has been reciprocated. I have, however, most certainly never asked or expected that as a penalty of your friendship for me you espouse all of my political, economic and social ideas or that you underwrite and approve of all my business and professional tactics.

I most certainly do not feel that there is any obligation of friendship that compels me to underwrite or signify my approval of all of your business practices. I am most certainly not sitting in judgment on you. It is entirely conceivable to me that every action you have ever taken in your quasi-public function as a contractor,   has been actuated only by the highest motive.. I merely say that I am not in a position to judge and have no desire or intention to sit in judgment.

I think I am as thoroughly Irish as you are. The fact that an accident of birth gave you a religious background from which my ancestors departed several generations ago, does not alter the quality of the blood-stream. Being Irish I think I have the same sense of appreciation of and loyalty to friendship that you have. This, however, does not alter certain basic facts. It does not make it possible for me to alter, if I would, the successful plan of an operation of an organization which is infinitely bigger than any man in it or associated with it. As I see it, no claim of friendship justifies you in expecting me to do the impossible.

Carl Magee may be right or may be wrong in his statements of fact relative to your activities in the contracting game. If he is wrong or has in any way or to any extent damaged you in your community, there is a way of redress open to you through the courts. But right or wrong, and your opinion to the contrary notwithstanding, it is my belief that Magee is functioning along the lines of procedure that have public acceptance as being legitimate. I am certain that he would not close his column to any statement that you might care to make, any statement within the bounds of reason and good taste. I can see no reason why, if he makes a statement based on this information, you should not address him or the paper in the interest of truth and a fair presentation of both sides of the controversial subject.

Sincerely yours,

John J. Harden, Esq.,
Petroleum Building,
Oklahoma City, Okla.

RWH:AML

November 20, 1928.

My dear Carl:

In a letter which I received from John J. Harden today, he en-
closed to me one of your columns which I am returning.

With the exception of one paragraph, which was purely personal
and which I have deleted, Harden's letter reads:

"I am enclosing you a clipping which Carl had in
today's paper. I have red penciled the portion in which
he states that I said, 'I am through with politics, unless there is some business in it for me.' This is
another damn lie, and probably one that was told him by
some curbstone politician.

"As to the rest of the article for your information,
and this is information that Magee could easily acquire,
at least seventy-five percent of the paving done by the
Western Paving Company in the past two years has been done
on my own property and assessed against my own property.
On this, we have paid the City an engineering fee of eight
percent, or something over $100,000.00 a year. I estimate
that this engineering cost the City about $25,000, so the
City has made a profit of probably $75,000 a year from my
operations. His contention in this article, is that paving petitions should be allowed to accumulate until there
is about 100,000 yards ready for a letting; this would
take a year to accomplish and in the meantime, no property could be developed, and the City would be standing still.
You don't realize that we are doing more business and more
to build Oklahoma City, than all the rest of the real estate men combined. I do not claim to be doing this for
philanthropic purposes, but even at that, all of us like
to put big things over and we don't always look at the
dollar profit that is at the other end of the line."

In my judgment, John should have addressed this letter to you
rather than to me.

The second paragraph contains a statement of facts which I have
no doubt you would have been willing to publish had Harden
addressed it to you. Inasmuch as it was addressed to me
personally, I do not wish you to use it or the statements
of facts therein contained without first asking or obtain-

Roy Howard even wrote to Magee to diffuse the tension. Courtesy John E. Harden.

ROY W. HOWARD
250 PARK AVENUE
NEW YORK

ing Harden's permission. I am forwarding it to you
merely as a matter of information.

As you very well know, I have no intention of intruding or
injecting myself into this situation in any fashion
or in any manner. I am not on the scene; I know nothing
of the facts or the governing conditions. I do not see
your column for weeks at a time.

John should know that there is nothing in logic or reason that
wwuld justify me even attempting to influence your judgment on a matter which is purely a local issue.

If he is unable to get my point of view, I am truly sorry. I
certainly am unable to get his.

I will ask that you consider all of the foregoing as confidential, as disinterested, and as being submitted to you
merely as a matter of information.

                              Faithfully yours,

                                  ROY W. HOWARD

Carl C. Magee, Esq.,
The News,
Oklahoma City,
Oklahoma.

RWH:WEV

cc JJH

P. S. - I am sending a copy of this letter to John Harden.

                                            RWH

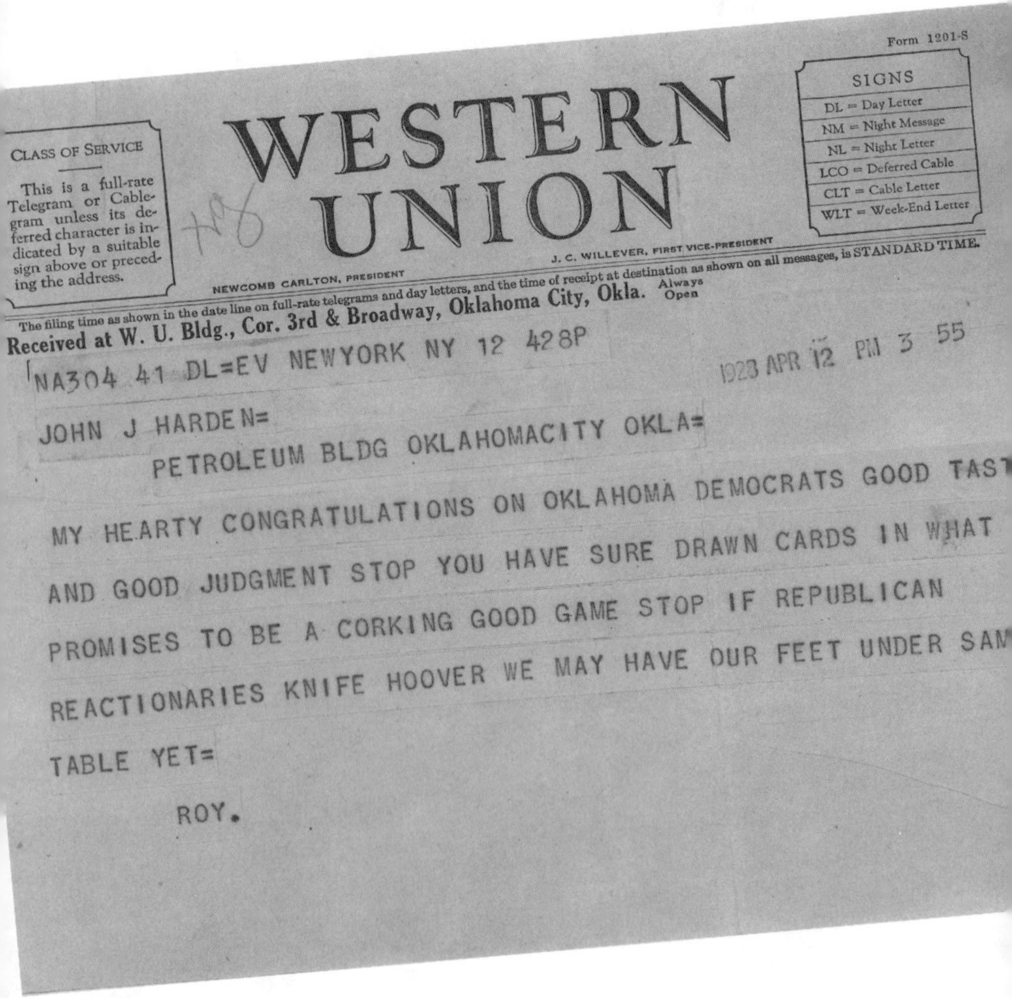

Form 1201-S

WESTERN UNION

CLASS OF SERVICE

This is a full-rate Telegram or Cablegram unless its deferred character is indicated by a suitable sign above or preceding the address.

SIGNS

DL = Day Letter
NM = Night Message
NL = Night Letter
LCO = Deferred Cable
CLT = Cable Letter
WLT = Week-End Letter

NEWCOMB CARLTON, PRESIDENT

J. C. WILLEVER, FIRST VICE-PRESIDENT

The filing time as shown in the date line on full-rate telegrams and day letters, and the time of receipt at destination as shown on all messages, is STANDARD TIME.

Received at W. U. Bldg., Cor. 3rd & Broadway, Oklahoma City, Okla. Always Open

NA304 41 DL=EV NEWYORK NY 12 428P

1928 APR 12 PM 3 55

JOHN J HARDEN=

PETROLEUM BLDG OKLAHOMACITY OKLA=

MY HEARTY CONGRATULATIONS ON OKLAHOMA DEMOCRATS GOOD TAST

AND GOOD JUDGMENT STOP YOU HAVE SURE DRAWN CARDS IN WHAT

PROMISES TO BE A CORKING GOOD GAME STOP IF REPUBLICAN

REACTIONARIES KNIFE HOOVER WE MAY HAVE OUR FEET UNDER SAM

TABLE YET=

ROY.

HARDEN THE POLITICIAN

John J. Harden's *modus operandi* in local, state, and national politics was behind the scenes as a fund raiser and power broker. From his early years as a business man in Oklahoma City Harden groomed and backed winning candidates for one simple reason. His real estate development and paving businesses depended upon having friends in high political offices. Government contracts made up a large part of the annual gross income of Harden's businesses so he naturally gave to, and expected from politicians.

Ironically it was Harden's religious beliefs, and not business, that made him "come out of the closet" in political confrontations. The anti-Catholic sentiments of the Ku Klux Klan and Harden's Irish Catholic background made him a "political bed partner" with John C. "Jack" Walton in the early 1920's.

Walton was Commissioner of Public Works when Harden moved to Oklahoma City. Walton controlled water and sewer lines, necessary components to Harden's real estate development projects. Harden jumped on Walton's bandwagon and helped elect him mayor of Oklahoma City in 1919.

Walton was one of Oklahoma's most colorful political figures. In 1922 he was elected Governor by a large majority. Harden raised money for Walton but stayed in the background because his major support came from labor and farm groups in the state.

Harden joined Walton's efforts to rid Oklahoma of the powerful influence of the Ku Klux Klan. The Klan had only limited influence in Oklahoma before 1921. However, as a crime wave hit Oklahoma City and Tulsa, vigilante groups were formed to punish lawbreakers. Night-riders caught bootleggers, dope-peddlers, and pimps and whipped them to within an inch of their lives.[76]

The Klan widened its purposes in Oklahoma City in 1922 and turned to the reform of lawlessness and official corruption. The organization professed the highest purposes, the purest Americanism. Unfortunately, the ugly venom of prejudice spewed forth from Klan rallies. Klan members were taught to hate Roman Catholics, Jews, Negroes and basically any one who was not white and native-born American.

Historians have often ridiculed Mississippi and Alabama for Klan involvement, but Oklahoma holds the dubious honor of enduring the greatest volume of Klan violence in the 1920's. Oklahoma City Klan No. 1 had a "whipping squad," charged with meting out justice. The squad was called the San Hedrin, named after the Jewish body that tried and convicted Christ.[77]

Harden and the Ku Klux Klan were naturally on opposite sides of most issues. Harden was an active supporter of the Roman Catholic Church and was a big target for Klan members. He and other Catholic and Jewish leaders urged Walton to declare all-out war on the Klan. Even though Walton's campaign against the Klan made him a national hero, the opinion of most Oklahomans was completely different.

Oklahomans feared for their civil liberties after Walton declared martial law in Okmulgee and Tulsa counties and set up military courts to investigate hundreds of incidents of Klan violence. Walton tried to convince his constituents that his actions were justified because local sheriffs and police could not, or would not, prevent vigilantes from punishing lawbreakers. The governor talked tough, telling a crowd in Madill, "If one of these masked men comes to your home after you, turn loose both barrels of your shotgun. . . and I will pardon you."[78] Walton ultimately lost his battle of public opinion and was impeached by the Oklahoma legislature.

Alfred Emanuel Smith, the Republican presidential nominee, during a stopover in Oklahoma City in September 1928. Harden and Smith were both Catholics and shared beliefs in the area of social reform and private enterprise. Courtesy *The Daily Oklahoman.*

Harden continued to be active in local and state political races. He gave money, raised money, and spent money for city council and mayorial candidates who could help him in his business. He became friends with oil man Ernest W. Marland, founder of Marland Oil Company which later became Conoco. Harden was one of Marland's biggest contributors and supporters when he was elected governor in 1934.

It was self-interest and political clout in local and state elections that prompted Harden to jump into national politics in 1928. Irish Catholic friends in New York City introduced Harden to Alfred Emanuel Smith, known to his friends as "Al" or the "Happy Warrior." Harden and Oklahoma City Mayor O. A. Cargill met with Smith during the 1924 Democratic National Convention and both came back to Oklahoma as fans.

Smith served as sheriff of New York County, as a member of the New York State Assembly, and four terms as governor of New York State. He had unsuccessfully sought the Democratic party nomination for President in 1920 and 1924, even though his nomination speech at the 1924 convention was made by none other than Franklin D. Roosevelt. Smith's advocacy of social-reform policies, women suffrage, and equalization of salaries between men and women launched him into the national limelight in 1928. Harden was attracted to Smith's pro-business and growth positions and pledged his support to his fellow Catholic.

Harden's contacts with the Al Smith campaign were Joseph Johnson, the New York City Commissioner of Public Works, and Smith campaign manager George Van Namee. Johnson and Van Namee were reputed Tammany Hall bosses in New York, part of the elaborate political machine that had catapulted Smith to the governor's mansion.

The Tammany Hall that eventually became an albatross around Governor Smith's neck began in the early nineteenth century as an Irish civic organization called the Sons of St. Tammany. The group became a party bureaucracy that "extended its influence into every tenement house, numbered 32,000 at its peak, Madison Square Garden had to be engaged for its meetings."[79] Tammany Hall became infested with profit-minded politicians and the society was hit with provable charges of corruption on and off for a century. Smith and his closest associates and advisors avoided any connection to graft and corruption but Governor Smith was eternally labeled as a product of Tammany Hall and crooked politics.

Tammany Hall was even interested in Oklahoma politics in 1926. Harden had introduced O. A. Cargill to Al Smith and his key people in New York years before. When Cargill announced his candidacy for the Democratic nomination for Governor of Oklahoma in 1926, Joe Johnson was delighted. Johnson said Cargill "has all the elements of popularity based upon his ability and fine and honorable character, to say nothing of his personality."[80]

Tammany Hall's support of Cargill in Oklahoma was part of a continuing plan to elect Al Smith as President. Harden assured Smith's campaign bosses that Cargill would be in Smith's corner, "I have Cargill's promise and the whole program is lined up so that the Oklahoma delegation will go for Al Smith instead of some Ku Kluxer."[81]

Cargill was defeated in the 1926 Democratic primary by Henry S. Johnston who was heavily supported by the Ku Klux Klan, which many people believed had control of Oklahoma politics. Johnston was elected Governor in November but was impeached before the completion of his term. However, Harden and Cargill were able to pass strong anti-Ku Klux Klan planks in both the Democratic and Republican platforms.

As 1928 rolled around Harden sincerely believed that the Klan was losing its hold on Oklahoma. Harden said he would like to find out if "it is impossible to elect a man to the presidency of the United States simply because he happens to belong to the Catholic Church."[83] Harden assured Governor Smith that he was running ahead of W.G. McAdoo in the hearts of Oklahoma Democrats. McAdoo, the son-in-law of former President Woodrow Wilson, had been Oklahoma's choice as the nominee at the 1924 Democratic National Convention. However, Harden said McAdoo's chances in Oklahoma for 1928 were much less after he (McAdoo) "had a meeting with the big Ku Kluxers."[84]

Harden promised Smith to personally finance Smith's campaign in Oklahoma in 1928.[85] In early February Harden contacted several Oklahoma City Democratic leaders and invited them to a meeting to discuss supporting Smith for the nomination. Harden reported the results of the meeting in a letter to Johnson, "A great many of the very best men in our City are with us and while it is going to be a battle, I am very optimistic in the belief that we will land in Houston with the delegation for Al Smith."[86] Harden met with *The Daily Oklahoman* publisher E.K. Gaylord and was convinced that Gaylord "is going for us beyond the question of a doubt."[87]

Harden recognized that two major issues, religion and prohibition, stood between Smith and a possible victory at the state Democratic convention. The Ku Klux Klan still controlled much of Oklahoma's election machinery and the Klan bitterly opposed Smith's nomination only because he was a Catholic. Harden decided to go on the attack for Smith and produce as much public sentiment for his candidacy as possible.

In a report to Smith campaign officials, Harden wrote that a series of campaign meetings and positive publicity had resulted in "a number of politicians who are afraid of their own hides have come out openly for him simply because we showed them we had a lot of strength."[88] Harden had told Governor Smith earlier that he was in favor of "a quiet fight" for Oklahoma's delegates but admitted that "if we had done this, we would not have had a chance."[89]

Harden was named treasurer of the Oklahoma Al Smith for President Club. Harden communicated often with Louisiana Governor Huey P. Long who was heading up Smith's efforts in that state. Long gave Harden specific ideas on how to raise money for Smith and how to fight religious bigots.

In early March, 1928 Harden traveled to New York City and met with Joe Johnson and other campaign officials. Harden notified Governor Smith that he would be responsible for raising campaign funds in Oklahoma, "We do not need a dollar to defray the expense of this campaign

Scott Ferris was Harden's powerful friend who served Oklahoma as a congressman and State Democratic Chairman. Courtesy Oklahoma Historical Society.

either now or in the general election. . . you have several real friends here who are willing to join me and furnish the necessary funds."[90]

In April Oklahoma Democrats convened to elect 20 delegates to the Democratic National Convention scheduled for July in Houston, Texas. Harden was a major force at the state convention because his business partner Scott Ferris was Oklahoma Democratic Chairman. As expected the ultra-dry forces and anti-Catholic delegates put up a big fight against Smith. Harden estimated that 1,600 of the 2,100 Democrats at the state convention supported Smith for the nomination over challengers U.S. Senator James Reed of Missouri and Congressman Cordell Hull of Tennessee, a long-time member of the powerful Democratic Steering Committee.

Harden and his cohorts scored a resounding victory at the state convention. A majority of the delegates voted for Smith but the delegation was given some latitude at the Democratic National Convention to caucus and announce its vote to reflect the wishes of the delegates to the state convention. Governor Smith wrote Harden on April 11, "The great news from Oklahoma has just come in and I want to express my appreciation, thanks and congratulations."

Harden was surprised by his success for Smith at the convention:

> We disposed of the Klan and Ultra-drys in good
> shape. . . when the steam roller got to operating there wasn't any
> stopping it. We have a very safe majority of the delegates for
> Governor Smith. . . It is also a great pleasure for me to be
> elected a delegate at large, as I had to beat our United States
> Senator Elmer Thomas for this place. We did not have the help
> of a Democratic congressman and, of course, our United States
> Senator was absolutely against us.[91]

In May Harden began planning strategy for the general election even though Smith had not yet been nominated. Harden invited New York City Mayor Jimmy Walker to come to Oklahoma and speak on behalf of Smith's candidacy, "You and the Governor are the only Northern speakers we will need here, but we are going to have a bitter religious fight, of course, it will be under the cloak of the prohibition issue, but that doesn't fool us here." Harden said, "My heart and soul is in this fight because I happen to be one of the Turks who has had to stay in there and fight the Klan from the beginning. I believe we have them licked and we want to keep them licked."

Former Oklahoma Democratic U. S. Senator Robert L. Owen became the principal spokesman for the anti-Smith campaign in Oklahoma. On May 8, Owen, an 18-year veteran of the Senate, wrote *Tulsa Tribune* publisher Richard Lloyd Jones with a spirited denunciation of Governor Smith and his ties to Tammany Hall politics in New York City:

The stealings under Boss Tweed were estimated to be from thirty to forty million dollars. Tammany graft provides a means for controlling the New York City elections...Tammany can pad the vote of New York with thousands and thousands of fraudulent votes whenever the necessity arrives. Tammany has become so skilled in managing the precinct vote and raising big money for political purposes...it has at last concluded to attempt to put Mr. Smith in the White House by their methods.

Smith has been in the service of Tammany for 33 years. He spent his life in and around the Bowery as a Tammany employee until Tammany sent him to the Assembly and made him Governor. He deserves well of Tammany. He is a product of Tammany, a disciple, and is now its leading power...Governor Smith is not to be regarded as a mere man. He is an institution built up by the Tammany controlling forces. He is subject to their influences and will assuredly represent their views for he owes everything to their support.[94]

Prohibition became a divisive issue in the Democratic party in the weeks before the national convention. Harden, who was often publicly and privately scolded for his excessive drinking, was one of only a handful of Oklahoma Democratic leaders who were in favor of repealing the Eighteenth Amendment which had prohibited the manufacture or sale of intoxicating liquor in America. Most Democrats wanted to keep prohibition and constantly attacked Republicans for inept enforcement of the law.

Harden felt prohibition distorted the role of alcohol in American life, caused disrespect for the law, generated a wave of organized crime activity, and created a unique American industry of bootlegging. In a caucus before the Democratic National Convention in late June, Harden was one of only five delegates out of 40 to vote against a resolution that supported prohibition but promised that the Democrats, if elected, would strongly enforce the law of the land. Harden told the caucus that prohibition laws were unenforceable and that government could benefit from taxes on legalized liquor. Harden's viewpoint would eventually be adopted by a majority of Americans when the Eighteenth Amendment was repealed in 1933.

Harden's leadership of the Smith campaign in Oklahoma drew constant jabs from Carl Magee in the *Oklahoma News*. Magee advised his readers not to underestimate Harden's abilities as a manager:

> He never follows, but always leads—whether or not he knows where he is going. If Smith should be nominated and elected, Harden would be found by 4 p.m. next March 4 with his heels on the table in the cabinet room in the White House, waiting to tell the new president how to run the government.[95]

Oklahoma's delegation to the Democratic National Convention began as a strong Smith delegation. However, support for Smith softened, due to what Harden called "Klan" activity. Anti-Smith forces wanted the delegation to caucus before it left Oklahoma City. However Smith supporters won the first round of the battle when state chairman Ferris announced the delegation would hold its first caucus at the Rice Hotel in Houston the day before the convention convened. In the end, however, Protestant church leaders, ultra-drys and members of the Ku Klux Klan undermined the strong support for Smith. When the votes were counted, Governor Smith had 10 and a half votes, Senator Reed had seven and a half, and Congressman Hull had two votes. The vote was a slim victory for Smith who had failed to get any votes from the Oklahoma delegation at the 1924 Democratic National Convention. He had been told by Oklahoma Governor Martin E. Trapp that he would get no votes from Oklahoma because Smith was a Catholic, adding "I am the Democratic governor of that state and I had all I could do to get on this delegation myself because I married a Catholic woman."[96]

Harden was incensed with State Treasurer R. A. Sneed, Secretary of the Oklahoma delegation, who announced the vote as 10 and a half for Reed and nine a half for Smith. Harden was "positively sick" when former Governor Charles Haskell announced to the convention that all of Oklahoma's 20 votes were being cast for Senator Reed. Judge James R. Armstrong, a supporter of Senator Reed, had maneuvered the vote change in favor of Reed as the delegates, "tired with the room getting stuffy and dense with cigar smoke,"[97] left the caucus room. The convention stopped while the Oklahoma delegation was polled. The neighboring New York delegation agreed with Harden's count of 10 and a half votes for Smith which would have, under the rules, given Oklahoma's entire 20 votes to Governor Smith. Harden caused quite a commotion by later asking that the Secretary of the Convention change the record. Oklahoma's vote did not make a difference because Governor Smith was overwhelmingly nominated on the convention's first ballot.[98]

BATTLE FOR THE WHITE HOUSE

The battle for the White House began in earnest after Smith was nominated by the Democrats. Secretary of Commerce Herbert Hoover was given the nod by Republicans with the blessing of President Calvin Coolidge.

Hoover's nomination was a blow to Harden's chances of winning Oklahoma for Governor Smith. The *Tulsa Tribune* and the *Oklahoma News* endorsed Hoover. When it was rumored that *The Daily Oklahoman* would endorse Hoover, Harden panicked and reported to Smith campaign officials that "a very serious situation confronts us here in Oklahoma." Harden was notified that at a secret editorial conference the *Oklahoman's* editors decided to go for Hoover. E.K. Gaylord, vacationing in Europe, had apparently sent a Hoover editorial to be printed in early July. However, Harden convinced the newspaper editors to hold off until August 1.

Harden secretly asked Smith's campaign manager George Van Namee to prevail upon New York City advertising mogul George Katz to convince Gaylord to stay with the Democratic Party in the election. Katz was a large stockholder in the *Oklahoman* and was reportedly strong for Smith. Harden recognized the power of *The Daily Oklahoman* by evaluating the situation, "This matter is so serious that I honestly believe that if the *Oklahoman* will go for Governor Smith, we will carry this State, if it goes for Hoover, I believe we will lose it."[99]

Eventually the newspaper strongly endorsed the Republican economic policies of Hoover, foretelling the landslide of Hoover over Smith.

Harden was so sure that Smith would defeat Hoover that he put the word out that he would bet any man $2,500 that Smith would be victorious in the general election in November. Even Smith campaign official Joe Johnson was helping Harden find takers for three-to-one odds. Johnson wrote Harden on August 1, "Please write me whether you wish me to place this money now at the best odds that I can get?" In the same letter, Johnson reported the campaign was going good, "We hear favorable reports from the South. The women seem to be kicking up a little, but they all must know that the thing they are trying to protect called 'prohibition' is a monster."[100]

Governor Smith agreed to visit Oklahoma September 20 as part of a train tour through Kansas, Nebraska, and Oklahoma. The first stop for Smith was in Omaha, Nebraska where his speech was well-received. Traveling by day through Kansas, hundreds of supporters waited at every stop along the route to greet Smith.

The candidate sincerely believed that Americans would not hold his Catholicism against him. He was jolted back to reality when his campaign train was met with burning crosses on the railroad right-of-way as it pulled into the northern edge of Oklahoma City. The Ku Klux Klan and other anti-Smith cronies had organized an effective and demoralizing protest against the Smith candidacy.

The burning crosses angered Smith and resulted in an instant change of strategy by the Democratic nominee. For months Smith had ignored the whispers and attacks about his religion. But before he ever left the train in Oklahoma City he vowed to change his tactics and talk openly about religion. His advisors told him to continue to ignore the fanatics and bigots but Smith could not go on pretending.

The burning crosses, and local newspaper accounts that former Senator Owen had bolted the party because of Smith's nomination, were so traumatic to Smith that he gathered his speech writers

Oklahoma City Mayor Walter Dean in 1930. Dean moved in the same circles as Harden. The mayor listened to Harden's ideas about the development of the capital city. Dean died October 10, 1952. Courtesy *The Daily Oklahoman.*

around him, tore up his prepared remarks, and wrote a new speech. He told a reporter that he would feel like a coward, unfit for public office, if he were to permit all the scurrilous attacks to go unchallenged. That long night in front of a typewriter on a moving train through northern Oklahoma was a turning point in the 1928 Al Smith campaign. Harden joined the Smith train in Wichita and stayed up with Smith until after 3:00 a.m. planning strategy for the big speech in Oklahoma City.

Smith arose at the crack of dawn and ate the customary bacon, eggs and toast. A newspaper reporter said he mumbled, "Glad to know you," through a mouth full of toast to the privileged few who were allowed to enter his drawing room until Smith looked up and said, "There's John Harden, looking like he's lost a lost of sleep, Ha ha!"[101]

Thousands of supporters, including Oklahoma City Mayor Walter Dean, met Smith at the Rock Island station. Smith chewed on a cigar and waved his brown derby as the crowd "rushed indecorously, demanding that Al shake hands."[102] An estimated 50,000 people lined the streets of downtown Oklahoma City for a parade led by national guardsmen on horseback in what *The Daily Oklahoman* called "the greatest political show since the days of Theodore Roosevelt."[104] After the parade Mrs. Al Smith was honored at a luncheon at the Skirvin Hotel. Frances Harden was on the planning committee headed by Mrs. Frank Johnson.

Governor Smith and Harden had lunch at the Huckins Hotel before Smith received reporters and supporters in the hotel parlor.

One of Harden's key contacts in Washington, D.C. was Oklahoma U.S. Senator Elmer Thomas, shown in this photo registering at his hotel in Philadelphia in June 1936. Thomas was in the City of Brotherly Love to attend the Democratic National Convention. Courtesy *The Daily Oklahoman*.

Harden had worked for days to set up a national radio hook-up for the speech through local station WKY. He bought radio time and newspaper space to advertise the Smith appearance at the Stockyards Coliseum. Harden was worried about Smith's safety so he hired a large Indian bodyguard and borrowed soldiers' uniforms for volunteer bodyguards to wear. Sergeants-at-arms were appointed to remove any one from the auditorium who was disorderly or interrupted the speaker.

Nearly thirty thousand people jammed the Coliseum which was normally used for cattle fairs and great revival meetings. It was the largest place in which Smith had ever spoken. The Coliseum, built at the entrance to the Oklahoma City Stockyards, was the brainchild of Oklahoma City Chamber of Commerce manager Stanley Draper who organized a special non-profit trust in 1927 and used personal credit ratings of local businessmen to finance the project.

The Coliseum had seen many a rowdy gathering but the Al Smith speech in 1928 was something special. There was a continual murmur that rose up from the vast throng of Oklahomans, so much so that Smith had to shout into the microphone. The Governor was angry and launched immediately into a defense of his religion and opposition to prohibition. Listeners back in New York feared for Smith's life because of the noise of the crowd. Smith later said much of this noise was created by one supporter about half-way down into the crowd who continuously shouted, "Pour it on Al, pour it on 'em."[104]

Harden sat immediately behind Smith on the Coliseum platform, flanked by former Governor Lee Cruce, U.S. Senator Elmer Thomas, Governor Henry Johnston, Democratic chairman George D. Key, and State Auditor A.S.J. Shaw.

Smith met head on accusations that had been spread by his enemies. He countered whispers that he was a corrupt machine politician by outlining his exemplary record over a quarter century. He boldly launched into the subject of religious intolerance, saying "anything so un-American cannot live in the sunlight." He lamblasted Senator Owen for leaving the party and accused Owen of using other issues to veil his religious intolerance:

> I have been told that politically it might be expedient for
> me to remain silent upon this subject, but as far as I am
> concerned no political expediency will keep me from speaking
> out . . . I attack those who seek to undermine [our institutions]

not only because I am a good Christian, but because I am a
good American and a product of American institutions.
Everything I am, and everything I hope to be, I owe to those
institutions.[105]

Smith called the Ku Klux Klan by name, charged that the Klan
was breathing the spirit of hatred to millions, and accused the
group of urging his defeat only because he was a Catholic:

> The world knows no greater mockery than the use of the
> blazing cross, the cross upon which Christ died—as a symbol to
> instill in the hearts of men a hatred for their brethren, while
> Christ preached and died for the love and brotherhood of
> man[106]

Smith said he wanted no Catholic to vote for him just because
he was a Catholic. He said any American who would not vote for
him because of his religion was not a good citizen. Smith was
loudly cheered when he said, "This country can not be successful
and divide along sectarian lines."

In his autobiography Governor Smith remembered his speech
that fateful night in Oklahoma City, "One thing I noticed about
Oklahoma was that the people who were for me were very strongly
for me and by the same token those opposed to me were most bitter in their hostility."[107]

Smith's appeal for religious tolerance fell on deaf ears. Just one
night after Smith addressed the somewhat hostile crowd in the
Coliseum, popular evangelist Dr. John Roach Stratton, filling the
same auditorium, captivated his audience with a fiery sermon on
"Al Smith and the Forces of Hell."

In the end, Governor Smith could not overcome the endless
barrage of anti-Catholic propaganda. It would be another three
decades before John F. Kennedy could be elected to the presidency
over accusations of being a tool of the pope.

On November 6, 1928, Smith garnered fifteen million votes,
more than any Democrat before him, but was swamped by a Republican landslide. Harden lost thousands of dollars in bets he

made on Smith. He told a friend that the money did not matter but he was genuinely angry at fellow Oklahomans who apparently believed rumors that if Smith were elected he would build a papal office on the banks of the Potomac.

By 1935 Harden had added awnings and
landscaping to the Oklahoma City Farmers Market.
Notice the "Dancing" sign near the top of the
building; weekly dances were held in the large
auditorium on the second floor.
Courtesy John E. Harden.

A FARMERS MARKET

The Oklahoma City Farmers Market was born in controversy in 1927 when Harden proposed to the City Council that he build a spacious building surrounded by sheds to house all of the city's fresh produce sellers.

Since 1915 merchants along California street had complained about the hundreds of truck farmers who backed their trucks and horse-drawn wagons up to the curb and sold produce directly to consumers. Merchants were irritated because the trucks and wagons on "Market Row" blocked the street. Commercial produce companies complained because of the unregulated competition.

Periodic flooding of the North Canadian River, and the infestation of rats that followed each flood, made the unsanitary market conditions unacceptable to the public.

Colfax Moulton and H.H. Trosper, both well-known vegetable and nursery producers, worked for years under the banner of the Oklahoma County Fruit and Truck Growers Association to organize fruit and vegetable producers.

In 1923 a group of business owners promoted an idea to build a centrally located marketplace. However the 1923 plan fizzled after the North Canadian River flooded much of the land between Capitol Hill and downtown Oklahoma City, including potential sites for a central market.

The animosity between farmers and businessmen grew more

bitter each year. A bond issue designed to build a city market failed to pass the test of the voters in 1924. By 1927 the City Council decided to either sell bonds and build a city-owned market or allow a private company to build a market. Into the picture came John J. Harden.

In June, 1927 Harden officially proposed to the City Council that he build an ultra-modern market with two hundred stalls for farmers and at least 40 inside stalls for businesses, with ample parking and paved streets for good access. Harden's letter of June 28 asked the City Council to designate the market an exclusive market and pass ordinances preventing the sale of fresh produce any other place within the borders of the capital city.[108] It was a bold and revolutionary idea to both the City Council and the people of Oklahoma City.

From the beginning Mayor Walter Dean liked the idea of private construction of a farmers market. The mayor spent at least one hour per week refereeing disputes among vendors and listening to businessmen complain about the hucksters and the smell of decaying food. Dean invited Harden and his lawyers to propose a specific contract to present to the council for consideration. Harden wasted no time. He owned the perfect spot for a market, five

For the first two decades of the century farmers sold produce from the back of their wagons parked along California Street. Local businessmen complained about the congestion. When the North Canadian River flooded, rats invaded the area. Catastrophic floods, like the one inundating South Robinson Street in the 1923 photo shown above, came often in the twenties. Political leaders wanted someone to build a permanent public market—outside the flood zone. Courtesy Oklahoma Historical Society.

blocks near the corner of Klein and Exchange Boulevard, part of the old Delmar Garden property.

Delmar Garden had been Oklahoma City's version of Coney Island from 1902 to 1910 when it was destroyed by a flood. A Greek immigrant, John Sinopoulo, transformed 140 acres of worthless, sandy soil along the North Canadian River into a wonderland for children and adults alike. The city's new street car system brought many of the 600,000 visitors to Delmar Garden in its glory year of 1905.

The park featured a horse racing track, beer gardens, roller coaster, ferris wheel, carnival rides, dance hall, restaurant, swimming pool, and a 3,000-seat theater that hosted the great entertainers of the day and Oklahoma's first statehood convention in 1905. Free concerts and appearances by celebrities such as the Apache Chief Geronimo signing autographs attracted thousands to the park each day from spring to fall. Delmar Garden was no doubt Oklahoma's largest and most fabulous amusement park in history. In fact it was the largest amusement park in America west of St. Louis, decades before Disneyland in California could lay claim to that distinction.

Harden used his extraordinary talent of behind-the-scenes organization to build public support of his idea. Stanley Draper, manager of the Oklahoma City Chamber of Commerce hopped on Harden's bandwagon. The City Council received resolution after resolution from business, labor, and farm groups endorsing the project. Resolutions from the Oklahoma City Trades and Labor Council, the Oklahoma Truck Growers Association, the Oklahoma Farm Wives, the Oklahoma Farmers Union, and the Oklahoma County Fruit and Truck Growers Association made their way to the desks of city councilmen as the time neared for a vote on Harden's proposal.

By August Harden's lawyer, future Oklahoma City Mayor J. Frank Martin, drafted a comprehensive contract for submission to the City Council. The stakes were high for both parties. Harden, through John J. Harden Inc., promised to spend at least $250,000 on a 120,000 square foot market to contain not less than 30 business booths and 100 8' by 16' stalls for fruit and vegetable sales. Harden promised to begin construction within 90 days of signing the contract.

The contract obligated Harden to build a fire-proof building with adequate heating and toilet facilities, and a refrigeration plant. A meeting place for farmers and fruit growers would be provided free of charge and booth rental was to be limited to 25 cents per day for the first year of operation. Harden promised to pave all the streets surrounding the market. An unusual clause called for Harden to deed the property over to the City of Oklahoma City only after he had realized a ten percent per annum profit on his investment, a mathematical bridge that has never been crossed. The city had the right to purchase the property after 1933, an option never exercised.

In exchange for Harden's sizable investment, Oklahoma City would promise that no other public markets would be allowed for 35 years or "the life of the contract." The City Council would also be forced to pass necessary ordinances to prohibit the sale of vegetables, fruit, meat or any other farm products anywhere else within the city limits except in retail stores.

In late August City Council sessions were stormy as council members C.J. Stevens and U.M. Baughman opposed Harden's plan, calling instead for the passage of a bond issue to build a farmers market. Stevens argued that if the city built its own market it would have to pay only four percent interest for 35 years, rather than the ten percent interest that Harden wanted to realize before deeding the property to the city. Stevens said he was opposed to any "private real estate promotion scheme."[109] Legal action against Harden's plan was threatened but never materialized.

Oklahoma City's leading newspapers split on the issue. The *Oklahoma News* opposed Harden and thought it best for the city to build its own market. The newspaper was afraid that Harden would somehow gain a monopoly on the produce market as it alleged he had on the paving and cemetery businesses. The *News* accused Harden of expecting large profits from a new wholesale district that might develop around the market. However the *News* admitted that Harden was taking a giant risk and that the city would not be out a penny if the entire project failed.[110]

The *Oklahoma City Times* heartily endorsed the Harden plan:

> We have seen the market squabble rise and fall with the public pulse for the last ten years. The Harden plan offers an immediate out... If some builder other than Harden had promoted the market plan, I doubt whether there would have been much opposition. There is no logical objection to a man's making a 10 percent profit... I may not like Harden's monopoly of city paving through the Western Paving Company or his graveyard operation, but my judgment on the value of the market house project should not be stigmatized by the personality of the man smart enough to offer a salable proposition to the city which offers a fair way out of a decade old dilemma.[111]

On August 29 the Council voted five to two to approve Harden's contract. Mayor Dean was authorized to sign the contract which had already been executed by Harden. The only change from the original proposal was Harden's new promise that the prohibition against selling wholesale foodstuffs anywhere else but in his market did not apply to milk and dairy products.

Harden wasted no time in launching the farmers market project. The day after the contract was signed by the mayor, workmen began staking off the property. Shamrock Cafe owner Pete Paschal was given the honor of turning the first shovel of dirt as ground was broken for the market on September 1.

The announcement of the construction of the new market building provided impetus for other businesses to expand or build new buildings in the area. Pete Paschal announced he was having plans drawn for a new cafe while Anderson Lamp Company began adding an additional story to its building on West Reno. Real estate prices rose to an all-time high within a five-block radius of the new market.[112]

The new Farmers Market in Oklahoma City (shown under construction in the photo below, in 1927) was so popular in 1928 that it appeared on postcards sold to tourists. Courtesy John E. Harden.

An aerial view of the market (facing page) just before it opened in 1928 showed the 2,000 parking spaces provided. Courtesy *The Daily Oklahoman.*

Harden hired the very best available carpenters and masons to build the new market which was designed by architect E. Gaylord Noftsger. Harden's brother-in-law William E. Harvey served as general contractor and J.H. Winnieberger was the construction engineer who oversaw dozens of workers quickly construct the Spanish-style two-story building. The walls were made of cement blocks manufactured on site by Harden's own Western Paving Company. The blocks were covered with stucco. The roof was made of tile and asphalt. The gutters and drainspouts were cold-rolled copper. Thirty-seven different Oklahoma City contractors and suppliers had a hand in erecting the market.

Surrounding streets leading to the market were widened and paved with asphalt. There was a large parking area and the 118 open-air farmers' sheds that surrounded the main building were more than adequate.

Inside, the new Farmers Market was first-class. Harden had written to and consulted with owners and builders of markets in at least 20 other major cities in America. He melded the successes and failures of other cities to make Oklahoma City's market the nicest in the nation.

The main floor contained 45 stores or business booths. Harden's daughter Jane ran a candy store called Jane's Kandy Kitchen. There was also a drug store, Dutch oven bakery, drink stands, vegetable counters, coffee stands, meat markets, a delicatessen, card shop, paint store, music store, potato chip shop, flower shop, and spice store. Patrons of a beauty shop and barber shop on the mezzanine had a spectacular view of the main floor. A popular feature of the market was a 3,500-seat auditorium that occupied the entire second floor. It was well ventilated with large fans on the roof. The auditorium became famous as a roller-skating rink, boxing arena, meeting place for farmers and other civic organizations, and a dance hall where Count Basie, Bob Wills and the Texas Playboys and Merl Lindsay often appeared.

Fred W. Winn had been handling advertising for Harden for three years and was hired as general manager of the market operations. Colfax Moulton, who had worked so hard for a public market, was named market master. Traffic officers were hired to direct traffic into the 2,000 parking places adjacent to the market and produce stalls. Boxing promoter Billy Gragg was placed in charge of renting out the market auditorium.[113]

The Daily Oklahoman said the building "represents the final fulfillment of John J. Harden's dream. . . for the people of Oklahoma City and fruit and truck growers."[114]

On its first official day of business, June 16, 1928, thousands of shoppers were waiting at 8:00 a.m. at the two entrances to the market building. Harden had heavily advertised that 15,000 bags of free vegetables would be given away. The supply lasted only 90 minutes. A ten-piece orchestra hired for the occasion could hardly be heard over the shrieks of anxious women buying fresh produce at competitive, bargain-basement prices. One producer made enough profit on the first day to pay his stall rent for a year. Another sold a load of rhubarb before 9:00 a.m. and was back with another load within an hour. Farmers and their families stood guard over long rows of green, yellow, and white vegetables.

By 10:00 p.m. when a big bell mounted over the market master's door signaled the end of the trading day, between 40,000 and 50,000 people had passed through the market. The *Oklahoma City Times* noted that every stall was occupied and every merchant transacted business in a "circus-like atmosphere."[115] The *Sunday Oklahoman* said, "With a grand rush that swept everything before it, Oklahoma City housewives swooped down on the new public market Saturday and made the world safe for the careful buyer."[116]

Harden had become a wizard at bond financing by 1928 and raised $285,000 to build the Farmers Market by selling 6½ percent mortgage bonds peddled quickly by the Wall Street firm of Herbert C. Heller and Company.

Harden had succeeded in monopolizing the farmers market business in Oklahoma City. And most everyone, from the mayor to Chamber of Commerce officials, seemed to be happy with this newest monopoly. The lone dissenting voice came from *Oklahoma News* editor Carl Magee. Magee surmised that the monopoly in the public market was part of Harden's overall scheme of monopolizing the paving and cemetery businesses in Oklahoma, "Strange isn't it, that there should be a relationship between the sale of a bunch of radishes and the control of the policy of a city and state administration?"[117]

Magee accused Harden of using the public market project to control a large pot of advertising dollars to influence the editorial policy of the *News,* which had been hammering him on charges of monopolization of paving projects. "Just now we are trying to find out why a paving monopolist had a hankering to sell onions."[118]

In its first year of operation the Farmers Market produced sales of $565,855. More stalls were added in 1929 and yearly sales skyrocketed to $1.2 million by 1931. The Oklahoma City Farmers Market was hailed as one of the most successful centralized distribution points for produce west of the Mississippi. By 1931 farmers and fruit producers came from Arkansas, southern Missouri, Kansas, Texas, and Colorado to sell their crops to the citizens of Oklahoma City and to brokers who set up shop along the railroad adjacent to the market property.

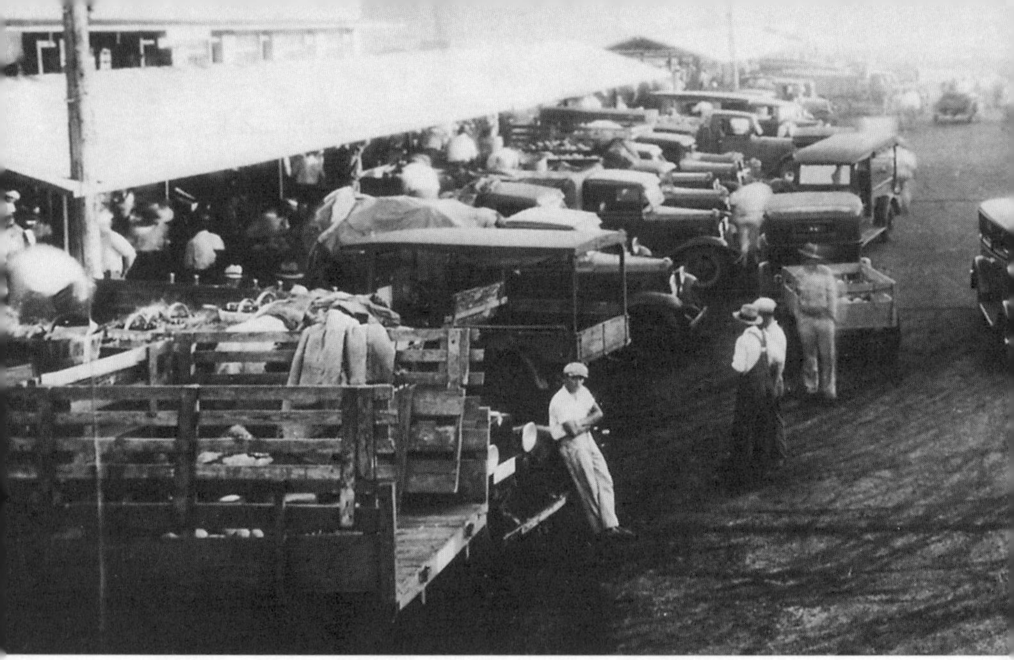

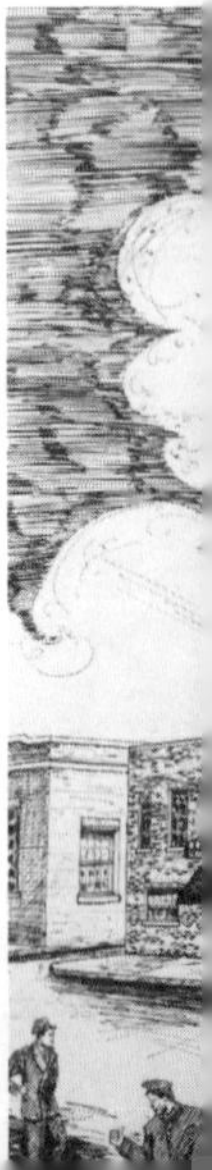

Harden's Farmers Market, top, was a beehive of activity during the Depression.
Courtesy *The Daily Oklahoman*. However, Harden's markets in Tulsa and Fort
Worth, above and right, never fared as well. Depression losses from the Fort Worth
market derailed Harden's plans to build more markets throughout the Southwest.
Courtesy John E. Harden.

In November, 1928 the City Council of Oklahoma City lived
up to its end of the bargain with Harden and passed far-reaching,
possibly unconstitutional ordinances restricting other farm and
fruit produce activity away from the Public Market. Ordinance
No. 3526, passed and signed by Mayor Walter Dean on November 14, 1928, provided:

That it shall be unlawful and an offense for any huckster, hawker or peddler to hawk, peddle, sell or offer for sale any food stuffs on any street, alley or sidewalk within a radius of one mile from the intersection of Exchange Avenue with Reno and Western Avenues.

An earlier ordinance, No. 3483, which became effective October 2, 1928, prohibited the establishment of any market south of North 40th Street, north of South 23rd Street or within the eastern and western limits of Oklahoma City in which booths or stalls were rented for the display and sale of meats, milk, vegetables, or any other kind of foodstuff.

The success of the Public Market in Oklahoma City spawned market projects for Harden in both Tulsa and Fort Worth, Texas. Markets in those cities flourished for only two or three years until the Great Depression hit and farmers could not afford to pay rent on space in the markets.

The Depression also took its toll on the Oklahoma City market in 1936 when the Oklahoma City Market Company, owned by Harden, went into receivership. Harden had assigned his interest in the contract with the city to the Oklahoma City Market Company which later merged into the Harden Mortgage Loan Company. The market emerged from receivership in 1938 as healthy as ever.

In the 1930's Harden badgered the City Council into enforcing the ordinances which prohibited the sale of produce outside the public market area. Several hucksters were prosecuted and paid small fines or promised not to sell on the streets again.

As the Depression adversely affected revenues of the public market, Harden looked for new uses of the facility. The large auditorium on the second floor of the main building was not used enough to make it profitable. As a result Harden had plans drawn to build 40 apartments in the space occupied by the auditorium, plans that never materialized.

In 1997 the inside of the Public Market building housed about 30 antique dealers and one of the state's best rare and used bookstores, owned by Jim Edwards. The building was 70-years-old and the large auditorium on the second floor was just a shadow of its former self. A time-worn sign advertised the fact that Bob Wills once played in the building. Farmers, nurserymen, and fruit growers continued to sell their products in outside stalls that extended for a block north of the market building. Several wholesale produce companies moved their warehouses to buildings that have been built over the years in a three-block radius of the market.

John J. Harden's grandson, John E. Harden, still owns and operates the Public Market.

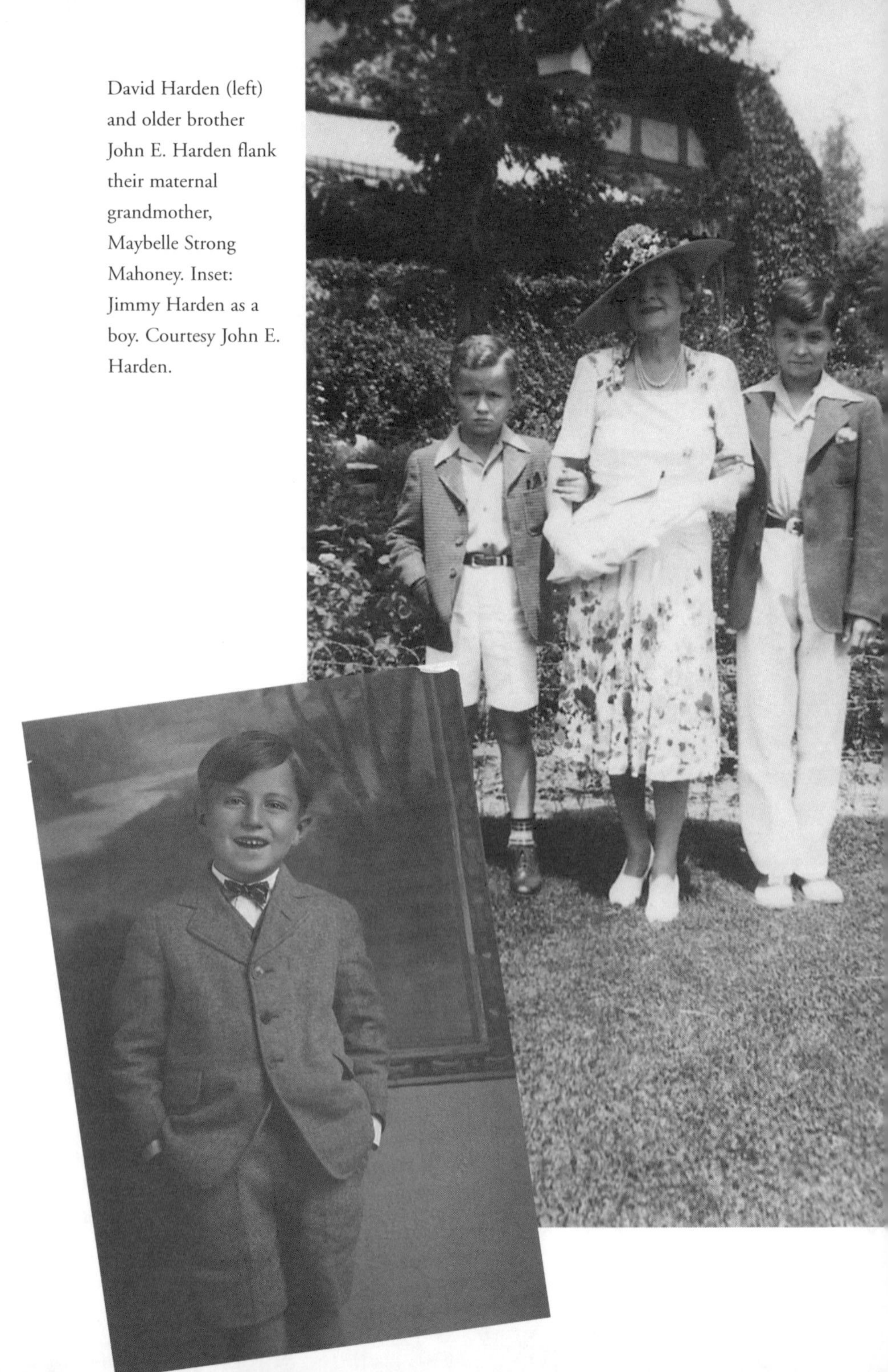

David Harden (left) and older brother John E. Harden flank their maternal grandmother, Maybelle Strong Mahoney. Inset: Jimmy Harden as a boy. Courtesy John E. Harden.

THE GREAT DEPRESSION

Like a heavyweight boxer who had been slugged in the stomach, Oklahoma was brought to her knees in 1930 by the Great Depression. It began with the stock market crash of 1929 and worsened as factories and stores closed, banks failed, and millions of Americans were left homeless and jobless.

Oklahoma suffered terribly when its agriculture-based economy faltered, causing farmers to leave their land to search for work in the cities. The economic problems on the farm were exacerbated by the weather. A searing drought hit the southern plains until even normally wet eastern Oklahoma was desiccated. Dust storms wracked the state. Sand blew in such quantities that airports closed, trains stopped, chickens went to roost at noon, and animals and humans alike suffered from lung disorders. All 77 counties in the state were designated disaster areas.

In 1929 Oklahoma's per capita income had risen to about 70 percent of the national average. By 1932 it dipped to just $216, half of a depressed national average. Farm foreclosures were a daily event. Oklahoma lost almost a million residents over the next 20 years because of the economic migration of its citizens to California and other states.[119]

As if the Depression was not enough, the coldest and iciest January on record hit Oklahoma City in 1930. For six weeks temperatures hovered below freezing. Ice and snow halted any home building or land development activity of Harden and his corporations.[120]

Harden had made millions of dollars in the 1920's from his subdivision development and paving projects in Oklahoma City. He had sold most of the homes on installment contracts. When businesses failed, workers were laid off and some had to give up their homes. Workers who kept their jobs were so afraid of the future they would not dare invest $500 of their savings in a new house or vacant lot.

A comparison of the monthly accounting records of John J. Harden Inc. tells the frightful story of the Depression's effect upon Oklahoma City's economy. In the month before the stock market crash in 1929 Harden's sales of houses and lots topped $75,000. However for the first six months of 1930 receipts for houses and lots averaged only $8,000 per month.[121]

Harden's personal income was affected by the Depression. His income in 1930 was $2.8 million, less than half of what it was four years before. Hit especially hard were his profits from the public markets in Oklahoma City, Tulsa and Fort Worth. Harden lost more than $100,000 in his markets from 1930 to 1933. Most farmers could not afford to rent the market space from Harden. Even farmers who could pay the rent were selling their fruits and vegetables to a shriveling number of customers wary of spending any hard cash.

A portion of the loss of Harden's net worth after the stock market crash occurred when the market for selling paving bonds dried up. The ready market of investors looking for paving district bonds simply did not exist as money tightened in the economy. Harden often had to discount his bonds by 40 percent to obtain cash needed to keep his businesses afloat.

As of January 31, 1930, Harden owned 10,000 building sites in seven states. He owned 300 lots in Clinton, Oklahoma. In Oklahoma City he held thousands of lots, large chunks of land in the Linwood, Crestwood, and Harden's 12th Street additions. On the books of John J. Harden Inc. were mortgages payable from homeowners and lot purchasers of nearly $750,000.[122]

The only way Harden survived financially during the Great Depression was by his extraordinary ability to operate a diverse group of enterprises. When the home building and subdivision business slowed, he stepped up the promotion of his cemetery and paving businesses. He crafted new ways of convincing Oklahoma Cityans that the future was bright and that they could afford small monthly payments on lots and houses. Unbelievably, Harden's real estate development business made only $40,000 less in 1930 than in 1929, dropping from $780,000 to $740,000 profit.[123]

Harden continued to spend large sums on advertising his housing developments. The advertising paid off by producing an average of 30 calls a day to the sales office.[124] In 1930 and 1931 he spent one million dollars on homebuilding projects in the Edgemere Park, Crestwood, Harden's West 12th and Linwood additions and started new developments in additions he called Meadowbrook and Meadowbrook Acres.

Harden announced plans in February, 1930 to spend $2.5 million to improve and develop 28 acres at Exchange and Western avenues in Oklahoma City. Harden's real estate sales manager A.M. Spencer told *The Daily Oklahoman* that the Sooner State Oil Company, A.W. Lee, R.J. Walker, Long Life Roofing, and Price and Sons Grocery were but a few of the commercial enterprises that had promised to buy lots in the new development once gas, water, and electric lines were installed and the streets paved.[125]

Oklahoma City's economy in 1930 was kept alive by large construction projects that had been authorized before the stock market crash. A one million dollar addition to the federal building was under contract. A Union Station for the Rock Island and Frisco Railroads was being built. The 11-story Black Hotel and the 31-story Ramsey Tower, later the Apco Building and City National Tower, utilized hundreds of construction workers who would normally have been out of work in other cities.

In 1930 Oklahoma City's population was 185,000, placing the city 43rd in the nation. Just one decade before Oklahoma City had been the 80th largest city in the United States.[126]

1931 was the toughest year on the financial empire of John J.

Harden and the economy of Oklahoma City. An official publication of the local Chamber of Commerce asked residents to advise their relatives not to move to Oklahoma City due to the shortage of jobs.[127] As America's economic downturn deepened, Harden's sale of lots in his subdivisions took a nose dive. In February Harden sold almost $27,000 in lots. In September he sold only three lots for $2,200. Harden wrote his brother-in-law, Vernon C. Hastings, in South Bend, Indiana:

> I did not feel the situation could get so bad. At the present time, we have not a single thing which is paying expenses except our paving company. We had a sixty thousand barrel oil well in Oklahoma City about 90 days ago and have not had a cent out of it yet. It is impossible to sell the oil.[129]

As usual the enterprising and innovative Harden turned to diversification for his investments.

Harden had health problems in early 1932. He thought he had a bad case of laryngitis when he lost his voice. Local doctors did not provide him any relief so he and daughter Jane drove to Palm Springs, California, hoping the hot weather would help.

After seeing three specialists in Los Angeles Harden was diagnosed with a tumor on his larynx. Lucky for him, the tumor was benign and was removed without incident. Harden wrote Roy Howard about his condition, "I don't know what caused it, but perhaps singing 'Sweet Adeline' had something to do with it. You can imagine what a helluva shape I was in, not able to talk."[130]

For years Harden and some of his wealthy friends had talked about investing in gold mines in the Old West. In April, 1932, Harden formed the Grand Hills Mining Company, a New Mexico corporation. He purchased gold mining leases in Arizona, near Santa Fe, New Mexico, in the Black Hills near Custer, South Dakota and near Battle Mountain, Nevada.

Harden sent his son John Hale to manage the gold mines, first to South Dakota and then to Nevada. John Hale took his wife Dorothy and their small son John E. to the rough mining country of Nevada to take over a mining operation that never actually made any money, at least legally and reported to the Internal Revenue Service. The price of gold was fixed in the United States and Harden's employees sometimes made runs to San Francisco to sell gold at inflated prices in Chinatown. Gold was also smuggled into Canada where it could be sold at higher prices, sometimes $5 more an ounce.

Harden spent $70,000 in 1932 to buy sand pumps, tractors, dray washers, sprockets and other equipment necessary to mine gold. He hired Chase E. Gish, a veteran gold miner, to head up crews of miners attempting to recover gold from mountains of ore.

Harden received much of his encouragement on gold mining from his close friend Rex Beach, one of America's best known writers of fiction. Beach held placer mining deposits in Alaska and urged Harden to spend as much money as he could spare on the Battle Mountain project.

Harden and his people perfected a machine that would wash large amounts of gold ore in the same way that a miner panned dirt by hand. Harden believed the machine would save 98 percent of the gold in the ore. He told friends, "It really looks like we do have something."[131] Harden ordered parts to enable him to build ten gold-ore washing machines. He worked out arrangements to lease the machines to miners in the Klondike in Alaska and to other operations in Colorado and Nevada. He was convinced that his machine could pan through 6,000 yards of dirt in a 24-hour day.

Harden, like many other American businessmen, looked for an oasis in the desert of the Depression. Harden wrote Beach, "I feel that I am fortunate to be in a position to buy and put in this equipment while everything else has gone to the devil. I honestly believe that we have the world by the tail with this machine."[132]

Harden's gold-ore washing machine worked great as long as there was an ample supply of water on a gold mine site. The machine used 500 gallons of water per minute in processing tons of ore. Since Harden's son was involved in the Battle Mountain mine, Harden had a tendency to micromanage the project. Day after day Harden wrote John Hale with specific instructions, "You better buy the pipe today...Why haven't you reported this week?...It

John Hale's wife Dorothy with the couple's two children, John E. (left) and David, in 1937. Courtesy John E. Harden.

looks like we will go like a house afire if we can just get the water. . . we still do not get the information from you as to why we get such small yardage. Does the water absolutely run out on you, or what?"[133]

Labor problems plagued the Battle Mountain gold mining operation. In the hot summer of 1933 John Hale was trying to make the gold mine profitable. He wanted his employees to work double shifts. He wrote to his father, "They rebelled and demanded 35 cents an hour."[134] The rebellion shut the plant down completely. After tap-dancing around the rebellion John Hale fired one of the foremen's brother-in-law, "It's good riddance. You can't have anybody's relatives on the job or they'll tell you to go to hell and think they can get away with it."[135]

The gold mine did not produce enough to meet payroll and

expenses. Harden subsidized the project monthly. When he sent another $100 to John Hale in September, 1933, he said, "treat it kindly because it sure is getting scarce."[136]

John Hale complained in November that his $100 monthly salary would not support his family through the winter, "When it gets colder we will be forced to buy coal, which our budget can not stand."[137] John Hale asked his father for another $40 a month to buy such necessities as clothing. He closed his letter, "Hoping to hear something encouraging on this little matter as soon as possible."[138]

By the spring of 1934 it was evident to Harden that his Nevada gold properties would never make any money. His expenses of operating the mine at Battle Mountain had risen to $1,500 a month. Often an eight-hour shift processing hundreds of cubic yards of gold ore produced only an ounce of gold. Harden drastically scaled back the operation and brought John Hale and his family home to Oklahoma City.

                                        December 15, '30.

Dear Roy:

        It certainly does seem that it is a long
time between drinks, and I have often thought about
my first meeting with you when I told you that I was
all through working and buttoned up on trying to make
any more money, or put in any new developments.   I
certainly have gotten entirely away from that idea,
because this really has been the big year on new developments, such as building a Public Market in Fort
Worth, Texas, and one in Tulsa, Oklahoma, and a new
town from the ground up at New Hobbs, New Mexico, but
even at that, I believe a man is better off keeping
himself fairly busy, than he would be loafing around.

        About two monts ago we got a seventy-five
thousand barrel oil well on our twelve acres adjoin-
ing Oklahoma City.   Two years ago it would probably have been worth several millions dollars, but under the present conditions of the oil market you could
lay down beside this baby and starve to death.   However, we are keeping the oil in the ground and one of
these days it will be a big money-maker.

        I am enclosing a clipping which I received
from your friend Jones, owner of the Tulsa Tribune.
I have also had wonderful co-operation from your
friend named Carter, and even better co-operation from
the Fort Worth Press.   Those boys are certainly on
their toes, and we are doing a little business with
them.

        Mr. Gaines told me that you were planning
on making a trip through here in the near future, and
I want you to let me know in advance, and I will go
to Fort Worth and Houston with you and we might promote some amusement.

        What are your plans for the winter?   I have
not made any plans yet, but Frank, Jane and I may take
a trip some place.

Harden chronicled the effects of the Great Depression in letters to Roy Howard.
Courtesy John E. Harden.

THE QUEST FOR A GAS MONOPOLY

In 1930 Oklahoma City's leading newspapers concluded that Harden held a strong monopoly on the paving, cemetery, and fresh produce market businesses in Oklahoma City. To no one's surprise, Harden directed his efforts in 1930 and 1931 toward another monopoly—the natural gas delivery system in Oklahoma City.

Cheap natural gas for residential consumers was at the top of the priority list of local politicians. Oklahoma Natural Gas Company (ONG) held an exclusive franchise to provide natural gas for customers within the city limits. The 25-year franchise had been granted to ONG by a vote of the people in 1909. Four years remained in the original franchise period when the gas company ran head-long into major public relations problems in 1930.

Citizens and political leaders alike were upset that ONG was charging residential customers 57 cents per 1,000 cubic feet of natural gas while customers in other parts of the Midwest were paying much less. Oklahoma City Mayor Walter Dean appointed a committee of newspaper publishers E.K. Gaylord and Carl Magee, businessmen J.F. Harbour and Charles Schweinle, and attorney Mont F. Highley, to investigate the high price of natural gas and to search for a cheaper source than ONG.

Harden saw the potential for large profits in a community that was growing even in the midst of the Great Depression. He played a major behind-the-scenes role in the political fight over natural gas, a battle that dominated local politics for more than a year.

Mayor Dean made it known that Oklahoma City was looking for cheaper gas for its citizens and that the City Council would listen to any reasonable offer. Harden went to work. He contacted his old friend J.G. Pundt, a wealthy Texas utility operator who had reportedly spent $14 million on utility company purchases in Texas in the late 1920's.

Harden's deal was simple. He would be the silent partner and use his powerful influence with Mayor Dean and the City Council to swing a gas contract, in exchange for one-third of the profit from the gas operation. Pundt needed only to come up with several million dollars to finance the deal.

Pundt offered to provide gas for Oklahoma Cityans for 39 cents per 1,000 cubic feet. Four other bids were also considered by the City Council. Investor's Utility Company, headed up by former Oklahoma Governor Charles N. Haskell, owned 13,000 acres of gas reserves in the Texas panhandle and offered residential gas at 45 cents. ONG recommended it be allowed to sell gas to customers at cost plus eight percent to provide a reasonable return of investment for its shareholders.

Southwestern States Oil Corporation, led by Democratic political leader Scott Ferris, bid 40 cents per thousand. City contractor Tom L. Green offered to provide gas at 36 cents per thousand, but wanted the city to appropriate necessary funds to build a gas distributing plant and lease the facility to him.

Only a trained observer of the political scene in Oklahoma City in 1930 could see through the tangled maze of Harden's handiwork in the attempted takeover of the gas franchise. Harden would have benefitted from the gas franchise being awarded to three of the five bidders. Harden had a secret pact with Pundt. Ferris was a close friend and political ally of Harden. Green entered into a secret agreement with Harden to give Harden 20 percent of the first $200,000 profit from the construction of the gas delivery system if Harden could convince the city to sign a contract with Green Construction Company. The handwritten agreement found in the files of Harden was written and executed on Skirvin Hotel stationery.

On Halloween, 1930, the City Council discarded all offers except the proposal by Pundt to build a distribution plant and give it to the city in exchange for an exclusive franchise.[139] Municipal counselor Malcolm W. McKenzie and Mayor Dean were authorized to negotiate a specific contract with Pundt. A week later on November 5, the council unanimously approved a resolution

JOHN J. HARDEN, Inc.

Builders and Developers

Real Estate

TELEPHONES:
CITY OFFICE 2-9131, 3-5831

OFFICE:
210-227 PETROLEUM BLDG.

OKLAHOMA CITY
November 4, '31.

Mr. O. E. Parker,
230 Park Avenue,
New York, New York.

Dear Deak:

I am enclosing a few clippings, which I do not believe you have read.

All through the life of the Oklahoma News they have worked for cheaper gas. In this battle they have made the greatest fight for forty-five cent gas I ever saw a newspaper make. We will undoubtedly be using gas in Oklahoma City within a short time at about thirty-five cents. I never saw a newspaper become so interested that they would hire automobiles to take the voters to the polls to put over a gas franchise. Of course I imagine the Oklahoma Natural paid for this, and the thought strikes me that if the Scripps-Howard newspapers are making combinations with public utilities, I want in.

I have just returned from Santa Fe, New Mex., while there I learned that Carl Magee had purchased a ranch there, he had also told his friends (all three of them) that since coming to Oklahoma City, he had made the trifling sum of two hundred thousand dollars—I think he exaggerated this about five times. He referred to the deal where he put John Nichlos, a man who had vast gas reserves, in touch with the Oklahoma Natural, and that this money was his legitimate commission. Of course John Nichlos had told Walter and myself that he had let Carl make $12,500 on some leases in Chickasha. Carl used the Oklahoma News and also his personal appearance with his arm around John before the City Council, which made it quite formidable. I would say that the News earned this money, and of course, I know they did not get it. I know you are going to appreciate my diligence in looking after the financial welfare of the Oklahoma News.

Shortly after Carl succeeded in putting John Nichlos and the Oklahoma Natural together on a million dollar deal, he immediately took up the cause of the Oklahoma Natural; having a boyhood friend by the name of Frank Long, who is Vice-President of the said Oklahoma Natural.

The street story (which I cannot verify) is that Carl got ten thousand dollars retainer, and was to get fifty thousand in cash if they succeeded in getting the franchise. Of course, Carl gives me credit for interfering with this deal, and it was beaten two to one.

I would like very much to have the bank clearings of Carl Magee compared with the bank clearings of one Deak Parker and Ted Evans, because these two boys worked on this paper at one time, and I know that they had no inclinations, nor did they attain any success in financial matters.

Of course, I am not expecting quick investigation of these matters, but I knew you would be laying awake nights waiting until I would give you the dope, and I believe, that if you will ask Carl about the gas transaction, that he has guts enough to tell you and the whole cock-eyed world, yes, that he made some money since coming to Oklahoma, but that this is his own private business.   Carl also made a very vigorous plea for the Oklahoma Natural over the radio the night before election.

Mrs. Harden and I spent a couple of days with Lucia and Walter and had a very nice visit.

With best personal regards, I am,

Yours sincerely,

JJH:H

granting the gas franchise to Pundt. The salient points of the contract were 1) domestic rates on a sliding scale from 39 to 15 cents per thousand, 2) no deposit required for domestic connection for service, 3) lines to be laid to consumer's home connections without cost to the consumer or City, 4) the City would own the distribution plant after construction.[140]

Business leaders hailed the decision by the council. Owners of the Colcord Building estimated that the Pundt contract would save them more than $1,000 per year.[141] The *Oklahoma City Times* editorialized, "It looks as though the Oklahoma Natural has sinned away its day of grace...After years of effort we are at last getting somewhere on the gas situation."[142] The *Times* editorial said all that the people of Oklahoma City wanted was the chance to vote on a cheaper gas proposition and the "difference between 57 cents a thousand and 39 cents a thousand means hard dollars in the pockets of every gas customer."[143]

The newspaper suggested that Mayor Dean and his associates be honored with monuments of marble for forcing a big corporation to its knees:

Relief from exorbitant gas rates in Oklahoma City is in sight. Don't let any smooth tongued friend of the Oklahoma Natural, which is fighting for its life locally, talk you out of it. Remember the Oklahoma Natural could afford to spend $500,000 to beat this franchise.[144]

Oklahoma News editor Carl Magee refused to support the Pundt proposal and wrote, "Something's rotten in Denmark."[145] Magee called Pundt a "professional promoter" and hinted that Pundt had been under-financed in some of his Texas operations. Magee charged that his input on the citizen's committee had been ignored and declared he would hold any final judgment of the project until Pundt was given a fair opportunity to obtain funding for the gas system.

Pundt began to look for financial backing for his project. The City Council decided to delay the call for a special franchise election until financiers assured the city that Pundt had sufficient funds available to fulfill his contract.

While the council waited on word from Pundt's bankers, the war of words continued. The *Oklahoma City Times* kept pressure on ONG to cut its rates, "A reduction of from 12 to 20 cents in the domestic rates is possible and we propose to fight for it until the finish."[146] Across town Carl Magee at the *Oklahoma News* somehow discovered that Harden was involved in the Pundt contract with the city:

> Why do we oppose the chance to get a 39-cent gas rate? We do not. There is no such chance. . . The hand of Mr. Pundt and his associates, Western Paving and Tom Green, is faster than the public's eye. That is all. It looks like the pea is under the 39-cent shell, but it is not there...The News insists that the city and the Oklahoma Natural get together and find a basis for an agreement. . . We demand that Oklahoma Natural be reasonable. We insist that the council be sensible. The public wants this matter worked out and settled.[147]

When Pundt did not return to Oklahoma City for three weeks

with financial backers in tow, city fathers became fidgety. So did the *Oklahoma News,* "The people ought to be able to see what a fly-by-night deal the council is trifling with."[148]

Harden desperately tried to help Pundt with financing. With the assistance of Pundt's local attorney Gus Paul, Harden attempted to secure five million dollars from August Belmont and Company, a New York investment bank, Stern Brothers and Company of Kansas City, investment bond brokers, and Jesse H. Jones, a Houston, Texas banker who later would become one of the financial architects of Roosevelt's New Deal.

Harden wrote Jones about the natural gas franchise in early December, "This certainly is a sweet deal, but I have had so many deals this year and have invested and borrowed to the limit, I am not in a position to put any money into it, but thought perhaps you could see some way to work it out."[149] Harden predicted that the exclusive gas franchise could show a two-million dollar per year profit by its sixth year of operation.

By January, 1931 it was apparent that Pundt could not secure adequate financing to pull off the gas monopoly deal. Harden approached other utility operators in the Midwest with the promise of using his political clout to obtain a gas franchise. The combination of tight money and ONG's conciliatory attitude to the idea of cutting rates killed Harden's attempt to take over the gas market.

ONG's problems were not over. The City Council set a franchise election at ONG's request for October 27, 1931. Harden, through his Western Paving, joined forces with E.K. Gaylord and *The Daily Oklahoman* to fight ONG's exclusive operation of the natural gas delivery system for another 25 years.

Gaylord was accused of opposing the ONG franchise because he was interested personally in obtaining a franchise, a charge that Gaylord flatly denied in a front page editorial on the Sunday before the election. The publisher called for the voters to defeat ONG and force the company to offer citizens a better deal, "Every citizen is entitled to a lower rate than 45 cents when there is an unlimited supply of gas at our door available at 2 and a half cents."[150]

On election eve the *Oklahoman* reasoned that voters had only two choices, "Do you want to renew this franchise and thereby practically end the battle for a fair gas rate? Or do you want to defeat the franchise and fight on until the victory for cheap gas is won?"[151]

Voters soundly defeated ONG's franchise request. A front-page editorial in *The Daily Oklahoman* was a seething indictment of ONG:

> The people have spoken. They have told ONG they are not satisfied to pay 45 cents for gas which the company can buy for 2 cents. . . They have said the history of ONG is a continuous story of exorbitant rates and arrogant treatment of its customers. By their vote they have condemned the gas company for its obstinacy in insisting on piping gas from foreign fields 125 miles away and refusing to buy any of the hundreds of millions of feet which daily blow into the air from our own wells.[152]

To its credit ONG reacted quickly to the disapproval shown by the voters. The company agreed to buy more natural gas locally from the Oklahoma City and Chickasha fields. ONG struck a deal with gas producer John Nichlos for large supplies of cheaper, local gas.

Gas prices went down in 1932 and ONG leaders smoothed the ruffled feathers of city fathers and customers. Ultimately the company was able to convince voters to approve a franchise for another 25 years of service. ONG weathered the storm and became a strong partner in Oklahoma City's growth.

John J. Harden (left) with Reconstruction Finance Corporation Chairman Jesse Jones at Encampment, Wyoming. 1930's. Courtesy John E. Harden.

HARDEN AND THE NEW DEAL

The Great Depression did not dampen Harden's superb business judgement, especially in the paving business. He owned or leased the only profitable rock asphalt mines in the state, giving him a virtual monopoly on the cheaper cold-rolled asphalt paving projects.

By 1932 Harden's Southern Rock Asphalt Company had exhausted the rock asphalt veins northeast of Dougherty. The mine was abandoned and Harden hired geologists to locate other rock asphalt deposits rumored to be located in Murray County.

Much to Harden's surprise an enormous deposit was found just two miles northeast of the asphalt crushing plant operated by Southern Rock Asphalt. The new deposit was leased by Harden in 1932. Southern Rock Asphalt filed a discovery claim on several hundred acres known as the Griffith Lease. R.D. Ross was the superintendent of Southern Rock when mining began at the new location on April 16, 1932.

The Internal Revenue Service required Harden to obtain an official estimate of the rock asphalt reserves located in the Griffith Lease. Petroleum engineer W.A. Krebs estimated that the lease contained almost two million tons of rock asphalt, a staggering asset at $4 per ton. Harden's accountants predicted that a net profit of almost $1 per ton could be gleaned from the new asphalt mine.[153]

One of the reasons that Harden had a "lock" on the rock asphalt business was that his mines in Murray County were the only pits in the state approved by the Bureau of Public Roads.

With plenty of asphalt to sell, Harden went to work to line up paving contracts in Oklahoma or anywhere a gravel road needed to be covered. When projects were slim in Oklahoma, Harden called on his powerful friend Louisiana Governor Huey Long for business. Harden was awarded contracts to pave hundreds of miles of highways in Louisiana. In New Mexico, Harden used his influence with Governor, and later Congressman, Jack Dempsey to obtain large paving contracts.

The profit margin was incredibly high on paving jobs using Harden's natural rock asphalt. A headline in the *Oklahoma City Times* screamed, "COUNTY ROAD COST TOPS STATE'S," when it was discovered that county commissioners in Oklahoma County awarded Western Paving Company a contract to pave May Avenue in northwest Oklahoma City at $12.10 per ton.

The newspaper was upset because a similar stretch of paving in Murray County was completed by Western Paving for $7.89 per ton, almost $4 a ton cheaper. Harden explained that the Murray County project was only a few miles from the rock asphalt mines and that labor was cheaper in southern Oklahoma than in the capital city. The Santa Fe Railroad entered the fray by publicly admitting that it charged Harden only 90 cents per ton for freight from the pits near Dougherty to Oklahoma City.[154]

County Commissioner Ed S. Butterfield defended the awarding of the 21-mile, high-priced contract to Western Paving. Butterfield said Harden's companies were employing hundreds of otherwise out-of-work Oklahomans and that Oklahoma County would benefit by providing its citizens with jobs in the winter rather than wait until spring to buy paving at cheaper prices.[155] The *Oklahoma City Times* called Butterfield and fellow commissioner Walter DeGraffenreid "crafty, impossible, and inefficient, and prodigal in the use of Oklahoma County money."[156]

Voters were tired of a depressed economy and overwhelmingly sent Democrat Franklin D. Roosevelt to the White House as their president in 1932. Americans, who were experiencing their worst economic woes in history, were open to Roosevelt's innovative measures designed to counteract the effects of the Great Depression. In 1933 Congress began enacting legislation to set in motion many new programs known collectively as the "New Deal."

Harden took advantage of programs aimed at putting unemployed Americans to work, spending a great deal of time on the doorsteps of federal agencies created in the New Deal. Harden made certain that any government agency targeting labor-intensive projects were fully aware of his paving business in Oklahoma.

One of the first powerful agencies created in Roosevelt's New Deal was the Reconstruction Finance Corporation (RFC). Its purpose was to make loans to spur the economy out of the throes of depression. Congress gave the RFC a half-billion dollars to start and Harden went to Washington looking for Oklahoma's share. Loans were made by the RFC to banks, mortgage companies, cities and states, anyone with a reasonable plan.

Harden was able to tap the RFC on behalf of his own companies. By 1932 he phased out John J. Harden Inc. and was using Harden Mortgage Loan Company as the official umbrella for his numerous financial interests. When there was too much publicity for Harden Mortgage Loan Company to receive loans directly from the RFC, Harden created Equitable Mortgage Loan Company which received frequent loans from the RFC, the largest being a $200,000 loan in 1933.[157] Harden's success in dealing with the RFC can be attributed to his close relationship to two very powerful men. One was Jesse Jones, his Texas banker friend known as "Mr. Ft. Worth," named by President Roosevelt to head the RFC. The other was Oklahoma U.S. Senator Elmer Thomas.

Harden had been on Thomas's campaign team since the Democrat was first elected to the U.S. Senate in 1926, and he was one of Thomas's chief campaign fund-raisers in his successful re-election bid in 1932. Correspondence files reveal a close working relationship between the two men. Thomas gave Harden early information on government programs that he might want to take advantage of. An example is a telegram from Thomas to Harden:

PUBLIC WORKS ADMINISTRATION HAS SET ASIDE TWO
HUNDRED MILLION FOR HOUSING PROJECTS STOP
OPPORTUNITY EXISTS FOR AFFORDING IMMEDIATE HELP
TO UNEMPLOYED STOP IF INTERESTED WILL SEND
ADDITIONAL DETAILS.

ELMER THOMAS[158]

Harden quickly responded to such information by often making specific and timely recommendations on how Oklahoma, and Harden's enterprises, could benefit from the glut of federal money being appropriated for New Deal programs.

In early 1933 Congress passed a federal Unemployment Act that was actually a three-billion dollar public works program to provide money for labor and materials. Harden's letters to Thomas sounded like modern-day memos from congressional staff members to their bosses. Harden gave Thomas instructions on who to call and what to say and why his position was the right position.

One of Thomas's pet projects was Platt National Park in southern Oklahoma. The Unemployment Act authorized projects for national parks and forests. Harden wrote Thomas, "I believe this makes it possible for the Platt National Park to buy material for the maintenance and repair of the trails through the park. I sincerely hope we can work something out on this."[159] In the same letter Harden urged Thomas to push banking legislation to limit the interest rate charged by the RFC to six percent, citing as his reason the fact that Oklahoma City banks were charging eight percent, "a murderous rate during these kind of times."[160]

When the U.S. Department of the Interior failed to include any money for rock asphalt in its announced project at Platt National Park in late 1933, Harden gave Thomas detailed instructions, "Go to Mr. Thom's [an official of the Bureau of Public Roads] office and tell him that you want rock asphalt on this road, as that was our agreement with him."[161]

Harden was desperate because he was running low on contracts for rock asphalt mining in Murray County. Harden appealed to Thomas to wire or phone Oklahoma Highway Department administrators on his behalf, [Tell them] "you are desirous of seeing the rock asphalt mines get a maximum of orders so the men can be kept working this winter. These people are really destitute, as there is no farming in the immediate vicinity, this is their only means of support."[162]

Harden used local government officials and chambers of commerce in Murray County to shore up his efforts to sell rock asphalt. When a lull in asphalt orders developed in the summer of 1933, Harden marshaled Murray County politicians for his cause. The Davis Chamber of Commerce wired Senator Thomas:

THE PROSPERITY OF THIS CITY...DEPENDS LARGELY ON THE OPERATION OF THE ROCK ASPHALT MINES AT DOUGHERTY WHICH NORMALLY HAVE A WEEKLY PAYROLL FROM THREE TO FIVE THOUSAND DOLLARS... WILL YOU NOT USE EVERY EFFORT POSSIBLE TO SEE THAT THE BUREAU OF PUBLIC ROADS WILL SPECIFY A SUFFICIENT AMOUNT OF THIS MATERIAL FOR THE ROADS TO BE CONSTRUCTED UNDER THE NATIONAL RECOVERY ACT PROGRAM... OTHERWISE SEVERAL HUNDRED FAMILIES WILL BE THROWN ON GOVERNMENT CHARITY THIS WINTER... [163]

Rock asphalt was unquestionably, in Harden's mind, the answer to Oklahoma's unemployment problem. He informed Senator Thomas, "If we are successful in getting the orders it will be possible for us to work four shifts of six hours each...this would employ approximately 1,000 men which would practically take care of all the unemployed in that section of the state."[164]

Harden launched a publicity campaign in November, 1933 to convince Oklahomans that rock asphalt on roads was superior to oil asphalt. After "a very favorable conference with Mr. [E.K.] Gaylord and Mr. Walter Harrison," the publisher and editor of *The Daily Oklahoman,* positive news stories and full-page Southern Rock Asphalt Company advertisements appeared in the newspaper about the benefits of using Oklahoma rock asphalt to hard-surface streets and highways.[165]

THE WPA

By 1934 Harden employed more than 1,000 men in the rock asphalt operation in Murray County. With high unemployment in the state, Harden's hiring ability drew the attention of politicians seeking jobs for their constituents. Harden used his charisma, his business sense, and the emotional appeal of taking men off federal and state relief to promote paving projects.

From the beginning of the New Deal the Federal Emergency Relief Administration (FERA) had awarded subsistence grants to needy families but its effectiveness was thwarted by red tape and inefficiency. National leaders, including President Roosevelt and FERA director Harry Hopkins, thought the gift of money was demeaning to unemployed Americans. In 1935 Roosevelt and Hopkins convinced Congress to create the Works Projects Administration (WPA), a new public works program designed to uphold the pride and self-respect of workers and still relieve their distress. It was directed by Hopkins and top administrators of the FERA. The WPA proved to be a successful and long-lasting public works program that left cities and communities with schools, parks, and bridges still in use more than 60 years later.

Harden courted WPA officials with a simple message: Rock asphalt mines and paving projects were the best labor-intensive jobs available in Oklahoma. Over the next half-dozen years few would make as much money from WPA projects as did Harden.

Harden also incited citizens of Murray County to promote his asphalt mining operation. In October, 1935, he orchestrated a massive telegraph effort by out-of-work asphalt miners to convince politicians in Washington, D.C. to approve cold-rolled asphalt highway projects. A committee representing the miners around Dougherty wired President Roosevelt:

WE REPRESENT 800 MINERS IN THE ROCK ASPHALT
MINES. . . WE HAVE ONLY BEEN ABLE TO WORK ONE
MONTH DURING THE PAST TEN MONTHS. WE ARE NOT
ON THE RELIEF ROLLS. . . AND DO NOT WANT TO GO ON
RELIEF. WHAT WE WANT IS WORK.[166]

The miners said Southern Rock Asphalt Company had always been fair to them. They asked Roosevelt to put pressure on WPA chief Harry Hopkins and U.S. Bureau of Public Roads chief engineer Thomas H. McDonald to designate rock asphalt as an acceptable material for hard-surfacing roads in WPA projects.

The telegram campaign worked. The Bureau of Public Roads stamped its official approval on the use of rock asphalt. Harden's asphalt leases in Murray County were the only locations in Oklahoma certified by the Bureau of Public Roads as meeting the strict agency specifications.

The WPA granted the Oklahoma Highway Department $18 million for road construction. Harden used his friendship with members of the Oklahoma Highway Commission to get his share of the money for rock asphalt projects. Senator Elmer Thomas entered the dispute between oil and rock asphalt contractors on the side of Harden and rock asphalt. Thomas wrote to Highway Commission chairman H.M. Arnold, "In this emergency, the Administration is looking with favor upon projects giving the maximum amount of labor; hence the rock asphalt top would be practically wholly a hand labor, pick and shovel job."[167]

Southern Rock Asphalt sold the Oklahoma Highway Department 36,911 tons of rock asphalt at $4.25 per ton in 1935. It only took Harden's miners a month to harvest the large quantity of asphalt from the Murray County pits.[168]

Harden called on his old friend E. W. Marland for help. Marland had been elected Governor of Oklahoma in 1934 and was guiding the Sooner State through the Depression. Marland's influence with his appointees on the Highway Commission obviously made a difference in the members' feelings about rock asphalt vs. oil asphalt black-topping. In April, 1936, Harden was awarded contracts on 61 miles of highway paving, over 40 percent of the paving portion of the state's WPA program for the year.[169]

Harden himself wielded major influence with Highway Commissioner Scott Ferris, a long-time business associate and close friend. Ferris lined up with Harden in favoring rock asphalt roads. Coincidentally, Harden and partner Roscoe Farmer personally guaranteed Ferris's loan application to the Reconstruction Finance Corporation to refinance his Cotton Exchange Building on the southeast corner of Harvey Avenue and Second Street in downtown Oklahoma City. Harden even offered to pledge $42,000 in paving bonds as collateral on Ferris's loan.[170]

When WPA officials questioned the high cost of rock asphalt, Harden bought full-page ads in Oklahoma newspapers outlining the benefits of rock asphalt. He pointed out that while the State had to buy $100,000 of machinery to construct oil asphalt roads, no equipment was necessary for laying rock asphalt. Harden said, "We work ten times as many men on roads using rock asphalt."[171]

After ten days in Washington, D.C. at the Mayflower Hotel in April, 1936, Harden reported his success to his son, John Hale: "I got an order for 55,000 tons of rock asphalt from the state and 3,000 from the county which made a pretty good day yesterday."[172] Harden summed up the fight with the oil asphalt contractors, "It is a continuous battle day and night."[173] Harden sold the state more than 40,000 tons of rock asphalt in 1936.

The price of rock asphalt steadily declined from a high of $5.25 per ton in 1928 to $3.95 per ton in January, 1936.[174] Yet Harden made large profits on contracts with the Oklahoma Highway Commission, cities and counties. Harden was a dreamer and thought he could employ 10,000 men to mine rock asphalt if only the state's business community would get behind him.[175]

In May, 1937 State Senator Allen G. Nichols of Wewoka authored a bill prohibiting the use of rock asphalt on state highways. Instead, concrete would be used on major routes. Where traffic did not warrant concrete, a new type of asphaltic oil, "held by many to be superior to rock asphalt," would be used. Harden abandoned his usual low profile to fight this threat to his lucrative road paving contracts with the State Highway Department.

The *Tulsa Daily World,* in its *State Capitol Gossip* column, called Harden the "angel" of the anti-road bill movement and suggested that Harden was financing the bill's opposition, "Observers are unanimous in believing that when the highway commission closed the door to rock asphalt as a surface material the same action might have loosened the Harden purse strings in an effort to defeat the bill."[176] Ultimately a compromise was reached and Harden continued to sell rock asphalt to the state.

One of Harden's most notorious WPA-financed projects was a statewide road program approved by the State Highway Commission in the summer of 1938. The *Oklahoma News* broke the story July 21 with a page-one headline, "Harden Slated for $1,380,825 in WPA Project." The newspaper called Harden an "asphalt czar" and "close friend of Senator Elmer Thomas," and suggested that Harden was about to "go into business with the WPA."[177]

The unique plan proposed by the WPA mandated that only rock asphalt be used on 361 miles of paving. State WPA administrator Ron Stephens said the plan actually originated in Washington. Highway Commissioner John Coffey said the WPA promised to pay $2 million of the $2.5 million total cost of project and that it was such a nice proposition, "we could do nothing but sign." [178] Highway commissioners W.E. Grisso and H.M. Arnold joined Coffey in stamping approval on the Harden deal. Arnold said, "You can't beat getting two million dollars for a half million."[179]

Harden's opponents immediately went to work to undermine the WPA proposal. Oklahoma Fourth District Congressman Lyle H. Boren filed an official protest with the WPA in regard to the requirement that only rock asphalt, of which Harden owned the only certified source in the state, be used to pave state roads.

Boren asked WPA director Harry Hopkins to consider all types of road surfacing materials "in order to assure that the state gets its money's worth."[180]

Hopes for the project were fading when the WPA objected to paying more than half of the $2.5 million to Southern Rock Asphalt for the rock asphalt material. The WPA had strict requirements that not less than 60 percent of the total cost of a project be designated for labor.

Harden went to Washington, D.C. and conferred with Hopkins. Harden's position was that his employment of 900 to 1,200 workers in the Murray County asphalt pits should be counted as labor. He called this sort of WPA labor "indirect relief," and suggested to Hopkins that his plan was the most labor intensive project available in Oklahoma. Harden predicted that the road program would employ up to 8,000 men in the state.[181]

1 4 6

HARDEN SLATED FOR $1,380,825 IN WPA PROJECT

$2,500,000 State Road Program Limited to Rock Asphalt; Highway Commissioner Says Improvements Suggested From Washington

By ERNIE HILL

John J. Harden, Oklahoma City asphalt czar and close friend of Sen. Elmer Thomas, is about to go into business with the WPA and sell $1,380,825 worth of rock asphalt.

Mr. Harden is now in Washington for the purpose of satisfying any dubious WPA officials that the $2,500,000 paving project—$1,380,825 to be spent for rock asphalt—would be a fine thing for Oklahoma.

Senator Thomas, whose flying trip to Washington during the campaign was responsible for a WPA wage boost of $10-a-head, also is at the national Capitol, in the interest of more paving for the state.

And Harry Hopkins, national WPA administrator, is expected to sign within the next few days.

Limited to Rock Asphalt

The big paving program provides that nothing can be used except rock asphalt, and who in Oklahoma but Mr. Harden's Southern Rock Asphalt Co. could mine and deliver $1,380,825 worth of the required material in short order?

The specification that crushed rock asphalt must be used on all 361 miles to be resurfaced is written into the WPA project proposal, and a notation states that all estimates were furnished by the Southern Rock Asphalt Co.

Strangely enough, the whole idea of spending $2,500,000 for resurfacing Oklahoma's highways and by-ways with rock asphalt originated at Washington, according to Highway Commissioner John Coffey and State Engineer Van T. Moon.

'Such Nice Proposition'

They said the first thing they knew—about two weeks before the primary election—Ron Stephens, state WPA administrator, popped out to the state Capitol and suggested resurfacing 361 miles of highway with rock asphalt. It was said then that the proposal originated at Washington.

"It was such a nice proposition," Mr. Coffey said, "that we could do nothing but sign. The Federal Government is to spend $2,000,000 and the state $500,000. And about $150,000 of our share will be taken out in use of our equipment and use of our engineers."

So, Commissioners W. E. Grisso, H. N. Arnold and Mr. Coffey signed and are letting Mr. Harden do the heavy work in Washington.

"You can't beat getting $2,000,000 for $500,000," Mr. Arnold said. "That's all I know about the whole thing."

The paving program will put Mr. Harden into business as a sort of subsidiary to the WPA. All of the 900 to 1200 men who will be needed in his Murray-Carter County rock asphalt mines will be taken from the WPA rolls.

2000 to 3000 On Roads

And about 2000 to 3000 WPA workers will be employed in laying the rock asphalt.

In the project proposal, the work of Mr. Harden's miners is figured as WPA labor. Figuring the cost of the rock asphalt this way, it becomes but $800,000 or less, since the labor of mining is considered WPA labor instead of a cost added onto the price of the material.

This sort of WPA labor is called "indirect relief." The theory is that if the 4000 men were not working for Mr. Harden and the state, they would be on relief.

So, they apparently figure, the Federal Government might just as well put that much money into rock asphalt since it will "indirectly" produce employment at the mines. Mr. Harden has agreed to abide by WPA scales and regulations.

Ordinarily, the WPA does not like to spend $1,380,825 out of a $2,500,000 project for materials. But Mr.

(Turn to Page 9, Column 3)

LOST HAT COSTS CITY MAN'S LIFE

Jacob N. Grisso Killed By Auto As He Stoops to Retrieve Article

(Editorial, Page 4)

A gust of wind blew off a hat and snuffed out a life last night.

Jacob N. Grisso, 78, of 1304 NW 16th-st, bent over on U. S. Highway 270, near Nicoma Park, to retrieve his hat after it had blown off, highway patrolmen said, and was struck by a car driven by C. E. Williams of Okemah, a special investigator for Governor Marland. With Mr. Williams was W. E. Agee, another investigator on the governor's staff and a former Oklahoma County sheriff.

Suffering two broken legs, a fracture of the right arm, and internal injuries, Mr. Grisso was taken to Oklahoma City General Hospital. He died a few hours later.

He apparently had been walking to a farm near Nicoma Park on which he customarily spent two days a week, patrolmen said. He operated the cigar stand in the Equity Building until retiring six years ago. His son, Jay Grisso, now operates the stand.

Other survivors are his wife, John P. Grisso, a son, and Harry Newton Grisso, a grandson.

Friend Charged As Auto Kills Man

Special to The News

TULSA, July 20—Leo Warseat was charged with drunkenness today while funeral arrangements were made for W. M. Bullard of Fort Smith, Ark., who police said was his drinking companion.

Mr. Bullard died last night of injuries sustained when he darted into the side of a passing car near Newblock Park while under the influence of liquor, officers said.

Cromwell Youngster Killed by Auto

Special to The News

CROMWELL, Okla., July 20—Three-year-old David Wylick of Cromwell last night ran from behind a parked car and was struck by an auto driven by William Brown Thompson of Okemah, highway patrolmen said today. He died soon after.

OUTLAWS ESCAPE IN RUNNING FIGHT

Shot Shatters Texas Officer's Auto Windshield

TWO GIRLS MARRY

HARDEN SLATED FOR HUGE WPA CONTRACT

(Continued From Page One)

Harden pointed out that much of $1,380,825 would go to producing employment for 900 to 1200 WPA workers at his mines.

John H. Harden, son and partner of the rock asphalt czar, said that he considered it doubtful whether his father's friendship with Sen. Thomas would help in gaining approval for the project.

"After all," said young Mr. Harden, "the senator and dad have been close friends for years. Every time dad goes to Washington he goes out to see the senator.

"But lots of people go to see the senator.

"Dad, of course, was one of the senator's staunchest supporters. If he had gone out and made speeches or contributed a lot of money to the senator's campaign, it might look different.

"This is just a fine project and I think the papers ought to boost rock asphalt."

If the project is approved, the resurfacing will use 324,900 tons of asphalt before Dec. 1.

When Senator Thomas left the city last week, he said he had several important projects to look after. The $2,590,000 paving program had not yet been made public. Mr. Thomas' friends here said they understood that this was one in which he was particularly interested.

Kill Two 'Birds'

Under the original proposal from Washington, there were no requirements as to what paving should be done. This was left to the state Highway Commission.

And the state Highway Commission undertook to kill two birds with one stone. It was decided that all of the paving would be limited to resurfacing city and town streets in some 50 counties.

The idea behind this is to gain the good will of municipalities and attempt to smother interest in the initiated petition circulated by the County Commissioners' Association and the Municipal League.

This initiated petition, already signed and filed with Secretary of State Frank C. Carter, provides that the state Highway Commission will get but 40 cents out of every gasoline tax dollar, instead of the 75 cents it now gets.

Several City Projects

The other gasoline tax income would go to county commissioners and to cities to help them with their highway problems.

By rushing in and resurfacing 361 miles of paving in some 100 state towns and cities, the Highway Commission hopes to satisfy many Chambers of Commerce and city officials. This, they hope, will be a palliative to the civic leaders who are dissatisfied with the Highway Department's work in helping cities.

Oklahoma City has a number of resurfacing projects in the program, including some work on NE 23rd-st. Also, there is to be some work on May-av near NW 36th-st and a number of other streets are tentatively included on the list that is being prepared.

Here's State Resolution Calling for Rock Asphalt

At the suggestion of WPA officials, the state Highway Commission met July 5—one week before the primary election—and unanimously adopted a resolution agreeing to participation in the $2,500,000 rock asphalt resurfacing program. The resolution, setting out that only rock asphalt may be used, follows:

"In view of the fact that the WPA has made a tentative offer to the state Highway Commission to participate in a resurfacing program of blended rock asphalt which is to be used on obsolete surfaces such as brick, old concrete and on newly-prepared bases on the state and federal system, the blended rock asphalt to be of state specifications, the WPA to provide all necessary common labor, the amount of the program being two and one-half million dollars ($2,500,000) to be divided between the WPA and the state on the following basis:

80% or $2,000,000 .... WPA
20% or $ 500,000 .... State

"By adopting this program the state Highway Commission will have available a large sum of money which would otherwise go elsewhere. This offer, if accepted by both parties, will afford a great amount of work for ordinary labor, starting immediately and extending through the fall season, will be an improvement which will be beneficial to the safety of automobile traffic, which work would not be available to relief labor of this state unless this program were adopted.

"The Highway Commission has agreed that by adopting this program involving $500,000 in state funds, it is not to place the Highway Commission further in debt but other items of present improved programs are to be postponed for such time as required to permit the accumulation of funds to finance this program. It is understood that state Highway Commission is to have complete authority as to the location of the individual projects included in this program as well as supervision of the actual construction and after this agreement has been definitely decided upon by both the WPA and the Highway Commission, the Engineering Department is to submit a program to the commission in the amount of two and one-half million dollars ($2,500,000) showing approximate costs of each item in the program.

Oklahoma State Highway Commission,
By—(signed)—W. E. Grisso, chairman.

Attest:
(signed) A. L. Commons, member-secretary.

The *Oklahoma News* July 21, 1938 front page story accused Harden of going into business with U. S. Senator Elmer Thomas to sell the WPA more than $1 million of rock asphalt. Courtesy John E. Harden.

W. E. Grisso — Harrpy Hopkins — John J. Harden

With original WPA estimates furnished by John J. Harden and his Southern Rock Asphalt Co., only the signature of Harry Hopkins, national WPA administrator, is needed to start a $2,500,000 highway resurfacing program in Oklahoma. An agreement-resolution, calling for the exclusive use of rock asphalt in the program, has been signed by W. E. Grisso, chairman of the state Highway Commission.

* * *

After months of reworking the proposal to meet labor-intensive requirements, the WPA approved a scaled-down version of Oklahoma's road program. The program resulted in Harden selling nearly 10,000 tons of rock asphalt to pave city streets and state highways in several counties.

POLITICS AND PAVING

Harden was a frequent visitor at City Hall in Oklahoma City in the late 1920's and 1930's. He was a major contributor in the successful campaign of Walter Dean for mayor in 1927. Harden worked closely with E.M. Fry who was appointed city manager when citizens of Oklahoma City approved a city manager form of government that same year.

The *Oklahoma News* attributed the change of Oklahoma City's municipal government to the people's desire to overthrow "the domination of Western Paving."[182] Later the newspaper said Harden and Western Paving actually won the battle and the war, "People thought that the new deal put an end to that domination. They were terribly fooled. That was the hocus pocus by which Western Paving emerged dominant in an election which was presumed to overthrow its power."[183]

Harden was falsely accused by Carl Magee, editor of the *Oklahoma News,* of personally guaranteeing a $15,000 loan to Fry to cover Fry's losses when the McAlester Trust Company, of which Fry was chairman, failed.[184]

When Magee was called on the carpet about his allegations against Fry and Harden, he recognized the error of his ways and allowed Fry to respond in Magee's front-page column, *Turning on the Light.* Fry was harsh in his criticism of Magee, "I submit to a fair-minded public that if the editor has made a false, reckless

statement as to this alleged transaction he has forfeited and is un-
worthy of the confidence of the
people. Either he should be de-
nounced by all lovers of fair play
and decency as a wanton and cruel
defamer, or I should be immediately removed from my job."[185]

Magee, never an apologist,
continued to lash out at Fry and
Harden, "We would like to have
Mr. Fry explain the curious Dick-
Dean-Fry-Western Paving affilia-
tion. Let him explain why asphalt
paving contracts are let in dribbles
so that outside bidders are shut
out."[186]

The *Oklahoma News* suggested
that Fry owed his job to John J.
Harden through a "curious set of
circumstances."[187] Fry had been

E. M. Fry was city manager of
Oklahoma City and a high official
in the Works Progress
Administration during the Great
Depression. He was a key contact
for Harden. Courtesy *The Daily
Oklahoman.*

an assistant to Robert W. Dick when Dick was warden of the state
penitentiary and later mayor of Ardmore. Dick's son-in-law, Bob
Finley, was a trusted employee in Harden's paving operations so
Dick constantly preached the virtues of rock asphalt. Walter Dean
was city engineer in Ardmore during Dick's term as mayor. When
Dean was elected mayor of Oklahoma City, Fry was chosen as city
manager.

Editor Magee admitted that Fry's hiring may have been a coin-
cidence, but told his readers, "We are just dying of curiosity to
know what the effect on the price and quality of asphalt paving
would be if it were lumped and let in contracts large enough to in-
vite competition."[188]

The *Oklahoma News* made Harden and his paving monopoly
the central issue in the 1931 mayorial and city council election in
Oklahoma City. The newspaper accused Harden of running City

Hall for the previous four years, "Western Paving took charge from the beginning. It chose the mayor and the city manager and the result is well known to every citizen."[189] Editor Magee alleged that paving costs were 40 percent too high in the Dean administration, "The whole set-up, from top to bottom, was dictated by Western Paving and its lesser lights."[190]

For some unknown reason Harden backed former mayor and Oklahoma Governor Jack Walton in the mayor's race in 1931 even though the *Oklahoma City Times* blamed Harden for the primary defeat of incumbent mayor Walter Dean, "The voters felt the ties between the Dean administration and the Western Paving Company have been too close. . . and so they gave Dean the coupe de grace."[191] The newspaper said Dean had been a splendid mayor but misread the temper of the public.

No doubt the voters rebuked the Dean administration by nominating Walton who was ridiculed by both major newspapers in Oklahoma City. The *Times* editorialized, "Our recollections of J.C. Walton's regime as mayor and his mad ride as governor, prompts us to hastily declare ourselves in favor of the election of C.J. Blinn."[192]

Blinn and four new members of the city council were elected by an overwhelming majority. The slate of candidates had only one thing in common, they all opposed Western Paving's domination of City Hall. Immediately after the election Fry was fired as city manager. A period of turmoil began with a parade of city managers. L.D. Abney served 17 days, John McClelland died in office after 98 days, A.R. Losh lasted only 114 days, Albert McRill was fired after 18 months, and W.A. Quinn could keep the confidence of the city council only 48 days.[193]

Somehow Harden and Western Paving landed on their feet after the defeat of all their candidates in the 1931 municipal elections. Within months paving contracts began flowing to Western Paving again.

John J. Harden took care of his friends. If they needed jobs, he either hired them or recommended them to other employers. When Harden could not help one Eulah Herr land a position with the State Highway Department in 1931, she asked Harden for a $100 loan, "I was out of work so long that I am so far behind with my debts that I must have some money right away."[194] Harden loaned Ms. Herr the $100. The yellowed note still sets unpaid in Harden's files.

Harden's close association with a string of Oklahoma City city managers allowed him to recommend people for city jobs. He wielded the same influence with the State Highway Department. Harden was loyal to his friends even after they left positions in which they could help his business interests. After Oklahoma City City Manager E.M. Fry was fired, Harden recommended him for various jobs.

Harden used his friendship with U.S. Senator Elmer Thomas to land jobs for his friends and associates. Harden was extremely influential with Thomas in the awarding of federal jobs. Harden's files contain many letters and telegrams successfully recommending men and women for jobs in the WPA and other federal government programs.

After President Roosevelt's election in 1932 Harden was the primary mover behind the unsuccessful candidacy of Oklahoma City farmer and National Farmers Union president John A. Simpson for appointment as Secretary of Agriculture.

NATIONAL POLITICS

Harden continued to dabble in national politics during the Great Depression. He favored another run for the White House by Al Smith. When Smith's chances of nomination appeared slim, Harden climbed on the Franklin D. Roosevelt band wagon.

In June, 1931, Harden spent a few weeks "drying out" at the Bill Brown Sanitarium in Garrison, New York, where he met Democratic operative Bill Babor. Babor put Harden in contact with James A. Farley, the New York Democratic state chairman who was putting together Roosevelt's campaign for the Democratic presidential nomination in anticipation of the party's 1932 convention. Farley wrote Harden, "I am curious about your State, and I would certainly enjoy meeting you and talking conditions over with you."[195] Soon after Harden met with Farley and pledged his vocal and financial support for Roosevelt in Oklahoma.

Harden and Farley began a long and close friendship. Farley was one of the strongest and most influential power-brokers in American history. He was Postmaster General from 1933 to 1940 and chairman of the Democratic National Committee from 1932 to 1940. Farley successfully managed Roosevelt's first two presidential campaigns. He resigned his posts in 1940 when he opposed Roosevelt's bid for a third term.

Roy Howard and Harden were both avid sportsmen. In the photo at top, taken at Encampment, they hunted prairie chickens. Howard flanks the group at right and Harden at left. They fished together too. Here the two men show off a string of keepers early in their friendship in the 1920's. Howard is at right. Courtesy John E. Harden.

In October, 1931 Harden was appointed to the Democrat's national fund-raising committee by Democratic National Chairman Jouett Shouse. Harden became one of the largest Democratic contributors in Oklahoma in the 1930's. When the national party declared a shortfall in campaign funds, its leaders looked to Harden to raise the deficit. Time and time again, Harden came through to solve the Democrat's fund-raising emergencies.

Harden's support for Roosevelt wavered as Democrats convened in Chicago in the summer of 1932. Harden's closest friend, Scripps-Howard chairman Roy Howard, was pushing Al Smith for the nomination. The Scripps-Howard newspapers openly endorsed Smith who was a last minute entry into the nomination battle with Roosevelt.

However Harden felt Smith could not derail the Roosevelt freight train with Jim Farley as its engineer. Harden urged Howard to "keep a line out to Jim Farley."[196] Harden correctly predicted that Farley was a key player in presidential politics, "I consider him very smart and I believe he is going to be a big factor in the final decision."[197]

After Roosevelt was nominated, Harden lamented the fact that Al Smith had not started running for the nomination earlier. Harden wrote Howard, "Al sat on his can in New York and let Jim Farley organize practically every state in the Union on the basis that Roosevelt was Al's friend and that Al did not intend to run."[198] Harden asked Howard to put in a good word for him with Farley, "I don't know of anything that I want of the Democratic party but I have been paying a lot of their bills down here for a long time and something might come up."[199]

Harden was appointed to the National Rivers and Harbors Committee by Oklahoma Congressman F.B. Swank in 1934. When Swank heard that Harden was supporting his opponent, Harden wrote, "The next time any guy from Oklahoma tells you that I am attending any meetings for any of your competing candidates, you tell him that he don't know what he is talking about."[200]

June 9, 1932

Dear Roy:

I was glad to know that Baker would be in
the mood to take the nomination if it is offered to him.
Regarding the Oklahoma delegation, we have a funny situation. The voting is entirely in the hands of one man -
the governor - and everyone of the men mentioned in your
letter is his enemy. Carl Magee is also on this list,
and believe me, there is nothing personal when I tell you
that it would be much better if Carl would not mention
Baker in connection with the presidency. In other words,
let's play this game by itself, and there is no animosity
on my part when I tell you these things. I want to win,
and if nothing happens, I think it will be lined up O. K.

As you know, Al Smith would be my first choice,
but I have realized for a long time that he hasn't a chance.
I didn't make any other alinements because I couldn't see
anything that looked half certain. I honestly believe now
that Baker is the best bet of the bunch, and as I have been
playing the Democratic end of it all these years, I certainly want to be on a winner.

(over)

Harden kept Roy Howard and his New York friends informed about political
trends in Oklahoma. Courtesy John E. Harden.

I do not think it is necessary for me to tell you anything about playing the political game, but I would do this. Keep a line out to Jim Farley. I consider him very smart and I believe he is going to be a big factor in the final decision. You are already contacted with Al and it is very possible that you could be the deciding factor with these two compacts.

The Louisiana delegation is also entirely in the hands of Huey Long. At the convention and at the right time, I think I could have a great deal of influence with him. As you know, he is quite erratic, but I have spent a great deal of time with him and know just how he can be handled. I also believe you would be a great help to me in doing this. It might take an evening out around Chicago.

Where are you going to stay in Chicago? I will be at the Congress.

I am returning the letters which were very interesting.

With best wishes, I am,

Yours sincerely,

JJH:HM

Scripps-Howard Newspapers

ROY W. HOWARD
CHAIRMAN OF THE BOARD
230 PARK AVENUE
NEW YORK

October 31, 1933.

Dear John:

I hope you will pardon my tardiness in replying to yours of
October 20, as I have been neck deep in an attempt which
the World-Telegram is making to put the skids under
Mr. Curry and Tammany Hall.   At the present time the
prospects look very favorable, though the election isn't
until a week from today, and a lot of things can happen
in a New York municipal campaign in a week.   I have
been a little bit deeper in politics this time than
ever before, and about the only definite dividend I
have gotten out of it so far is an appreciation of the
fact that bad as newspapermen are in their unwillingness
to give a sucker competitor a break, they are big-hearted
and generous compared to politicians, whose idea is that
every opponent wears his belt around his knees, and that
any blow from the patella up is legitimate.

I was glad to hear that the obsequies had been said over the
law suit which seemed to cause so much worry to our
mutual friends while you and I were off on a hunting
expedition together.   And speaking of hunting:

I got back last week from a little ten-day party up in the
Laurentian Mountains north of Quebec, in the course of
which I managed to get myself a four hundred pound black
bear.   Karl Bickel, who was with me, knocked over an
aged and none-too-well-horned moose.   He was edible
(I mean the moose, not Bickel) even though not very
decorative.

Am happy to say that things are coming along very well indeed
with the concern as a whole, and especially well with the
World-Telegram.

Jack is back, and though he's been working in New York for a
few weeks, has not definitely located himself, as I think
he wants to get placed somewhere out in the Middlewest
on a smaller paper where he'll stand to get a little
more varied experience than is open to a fellow on one
of these highly departmentalized New York papers.

Hope the next time you get to Washington to touch our Uncle
    Sam for another loan, you'll find an opportunity to run
    on up to New York.

In the meantime, with kindest personal regards to you and your
    family from me and mine, I am,

Cordially yours,

J. J. Harden, Esq.,
Petroleum Building,
Oklahoma City, Okla.

RWH:B

In 1936 Harden was elevated to the position of state finance director in Oklahoma for the Democratic National Committee. Harden was influential in convincing Roy Howard to back Roosevelt's renomination and reelection. Roosevelt and Jim Farley both were impressed with Harden's efforts. Harden accepted the praises of the president and his campaign manager, but said he did not want any special favors in return. Privately, Harden fully expected to call upon the Roosevelt administration to help him promote his businesses, especially the pursuit of paving contracts handed out by government agencies.

Harden was also named chairman of the state finance committee of the Oklahoma Democratic party. He described his dual role as "a hell of a job." In an October 22, 1936 report to national Democratic leaders, Harden bemoaned the indictment of several large Democratic contributors in Oklahoma, "The government indicted most all of the oil officials in Oklahoma who were our biggest contributors so I had to put on a campaign and go out after the small contributors. We have an organization of about 1,000 working and it is going over in fine shape."[201]

When Roosevelt was reelected over Republican Alf Landon of Kansas in November, 1936, Harden wired the President at Hyde Park, New York:

CONGRATULATIONS FOR THE MARVELOUS VICTORY. . . I BELIEVE YOU COULD HAVE PROBABLY WON THIS ELECTION IF YOU HAD BEEN STANDING ON YOUR HEAD...I HEARD EVERY ONE OF YOUR SPEECHES AND I DON'T BELIEVE YOU MADE A SINGLE MISTAKE EVEN WHEN YOU TOLD SOME OF OUR MOST BITTER OPPONENTS THAT YOU WERE INCLINED TO BE MASTER OF THE SITUATION FOR THE NEXT FOUR YEARS.[202]

Roosevelt's national campaign was a half-million dollars in the red after the victory celebrations ended. W. Forbes Morgan, the national treasurer of the Democratic party, called on Harden to quickly raise $10,000 as Oklahoma's share of the deficit. Harden put a hold on his business pursuits and raised the money for the national party within a few days.[203]

Harden's involvement with raising campaign funds for the ruling party in Oklahoma gave him clout with almost all elected officials. He assisted Congressman Wilburn Cartwright in passing legislation in 1940 that authorized $300 million for public road construction in the United States.[204] Harden was instrumental in the election of Scott Ferris as one of Oklahoma's representative on the Democratic National Committee. When Ferris was struggling in his ownership of the Cotton Exchange office building, it was Harden who convinced officials in Washington, D.C. to locate federal agencies in Ferris's building.[205]

Harden's voice was heard loud and clear in matters of hiring and firing government workers. In February, 1936, Harden successfully manipulated the firing of Cy Avery as Public Roads Supervisor for the WPA in Oklahoma. Harden wired Oklahoma Congressman Jack Nichols, "I believe now is the time to definitely get rid of Cy Avery."[206]

Harden did not hesitate to let his feelings be known to politicians. A potential competitor in the rock asphalt business attempted to obtain a loan from the Reconstruction Finance Corporation (RFC) in 1935. Harden alerted RFC officials, referring to the man as "a wild eyed promoter. . . who was thrown out of the Mayflower Hotel and could not pay his bill."[207] Harden admonished the RFC to "not waste any time on a proposition of this character."[208]

Through U.S. Senator Elmer Thomas, Harden controlled many federal government jobs in the 1930's. Joe H. Condon was hired by the Federal Housing Administration (FHA) in Oklahoma City only after Harden and Thomas endorsed him in letters to FHA Administrator Stewart McDonald.

Harden kept Thomas informed on the political activity of federal workers in Oklahoma. In a January, 1937 letter to Thomas, Harden wrote, "In the collection of funds for the national and state campaigns, I received 100 percent cooperation from some of the departments, and they now call on me to let it be known to the U.S. Senators that they were of assistance."[210] About one L.W. Cozart who needed a job, Harden wrote Thomas, "He worked real hard in your campaign and is entitled to something. He will take a job anywhere, anyplace."[211]

Harden's close relationship with Thomas is evidenced by the contents of Harden's telegram sent to the Mayflower Market, located across the street from the Mayflower Hotel, in Washington, D.C. two days before Christmas in 1937:

KINDLY DELIVER TWELVE QUARTS OF YOUR BEST THREE DOLLARS FIFTY CENT PER BOTTLE SCOTCH WHISKEY TO THE APARTMENT OF SENATOR ELMER THOMAS OF OKLAHOMA AND SEND BILL TO ME. IF YOU HAVEN'T ALREADY DONE SO YOU CAN ASCERTAIN MY CREDIT BY CALLING THE CASHIER OF THE MAYFLOWER HOTEL.[212]

Harden also reported regularly to Harry L. Hopkins, Director of the WPA. Hopkins was a close and influential political adviser to President Roosevelt. He managed New York's relief efforts when Roosevelt was governor and headed up both the Federal Emergency Relief Administration and the WPA before being appointed Secretary of Commerce by Roosevelt in 1938.

Hopkins was one of the architects of the New Deal and was interested in how the New Deal was doing in Oklahoma. He often requested updates from Harden. After Oklahoma's Democratic primary in July, 1938, Harden reported, "Senator Thomas will win by over 50,000 votes. It is really a four way victory for the New Deal. Bill Murray is defeated by Red Phillips, who will make a good governor and I feel certain he will cooperate 100 percent with the national administration. Gomer Smith is out...and replaced by Mike Monroney, a very fine young man and 100 percent New Deal."[213]

Harden assured Hopkins that the WPA made a difference in the Oklahoma election, "Without your cooperation this could have been a different story. . . the two men who were in Oklahoma out of the Washington office took care of the situation in perfect shape."[214] Harden said, "I think that Oklahoma told the cockeyed world that the New Deal is in to stay."[215]

Harden hosted a visit to Oklahoma City by Postmaster General James Farley in May, 1937. Harden introduced Farley to an impressive group of oil men who were capable of making large donations to the Democratic party. After Farley returned to Washington, D.C. he wrote Harden, "I am wondering if anything can be done quietly among the group."[216] Harden sent Farley $1,000 for the national party and reported to Farley that he advised the oil men to send their checks directly to Farley at the Mayflower Hotel in Washington. Harden was not overly optimistic, "My private opinion is that they will talk big and bet little."[217]

Harden played a significant role in the federal judicial appointment of Oklahoma City lawyer Alfred Paul "Fish" Murrah in 1937. In June, 1936, Congress created a fourth federal judge position in Oklahoma. The new judge would be a roving jurist in all three of the state's federal districts. Some 40 lawyers and judges vied for the job, including Murrah who had been active in the successful campaign of Josh Lee to unseat U.S. Senator Thomas P. Gore.

Elmer Thomas was the state's senior senator and normally his recommendation to Democratic President Roosevelt on the subject of federal judgeships would have carried enormous weight. However, Thomas's term would expire in 1938 and he needed the support of the tremendous organization that Lee had put together in the 1936 campaign. Thomas deferred to Senator-elect Lee whose first choice was Murrah.

Harden entered the picture when Murrah, who had represented Harden and his corporations in legal matters, asked him to use his influence with Senator Thomas. Murrah was not Thomas's first choice but Harden and other business and political leaders convinced Thomas that Murrah was the best man for the job.

An intensive telegram and letter-writing campaign to Thomas was successful. Thomas later wrote that it was impossible to "hold out against his [Murrah's] appointment" in the face of "the endorsement and support of every major organization in the state."[219] In early February, 1937, Harden wired Murrah in Washington, D.C. that he had been told by Thomas that Murrah's nomination would be sent to the U.S. Senate. When the prediction came true, Murrah expressed his appreciation to Harden in a telegram, "IT IS IN THE BAG. THANKS. FISH."[220]

Within weeks Murrah was confirmed by the Senate and began his duties as a roving judge in the eastern, northern, and western districts of Oklahoma. Three years later he was appointed by President Roosevelt as a judge of the United States Court of Appeals

CLASS OF SERVICE DESIRED	
DOMESTIC	CABLE
TELEGRAM	FULL RATE
DAY LETTER	DEFERRED
NIGHT MESSAGE	NIGHT LETTER
NIGHT LETTER	SHIP RADIOGRAM

Patrons should check class of service desired; otherwise message will be transmitted as a full-rate communication.

COPY OF
WESTERN UNION TELEGRAM

Oklahoma City, Okla.
Feb. 8, 1937

A. P. MURRAH,
ROLLEY HOTEL
WASHINGTON, D. C.

IT LOOKS TO ME LIKE EVERYTHING IS IN THE BAG AND I CERTAINLY WANT TO CONGRATULATE YOU STOP I HAVE BEEN IN CALIFORNIA FOR THE PAST TEN DAYS ATTENDING THE FUNERAL OF MY FATHER AND I SINCERELY HOPE THAT YOUR APPOINTMENT WILL BE MADE WITHIN THE NEXT FEW DAYS

JOHN J. HARDEN

PAID.
CHG. SOUTHERN ROCK ASPHALT COMPANY

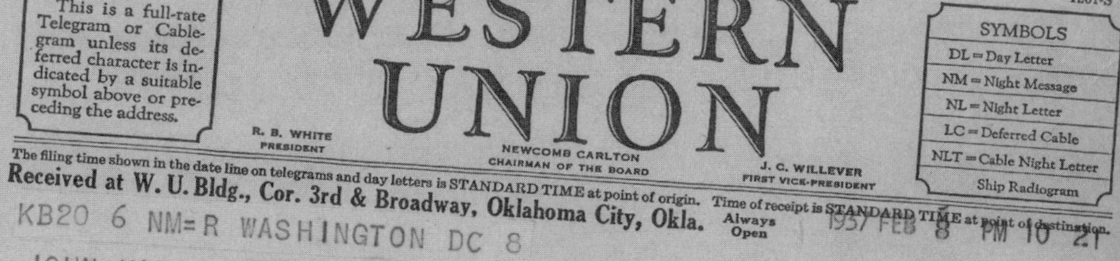

for the Tenth Circuit, a position Murrah held for 30 years. He became one of America's outstanding jurists. His name was broadcast around the world after the Alfred P. Murrah Federal Building in Oklahoma City was destroyed by a bomb April 19, 1995.

Harden (second from left, standing) was a frequent visitor to the
Pawnee County ranch owned by Major Gordon Lillie, otherwise
known as "Pawnee Bill," (front center in dark topcoat). To the left of
Lillie is Roy Howard. Courtesy John E. Harden.

THE CONSUMMATE HOST

The only things in life that Harden liked better than a lucrative business deal was a good fishing trip or a successful hunt. Much of his spare time was spent planning elaborate vacations to some favorite fishing hole or hunting preserve. Harden, known to his friends as "Jack", never fished or hunted alone. He needed friends nearby to make his leisure time complete.

Harden was a natural host. He was in his comfort zone whether hosting a wild party in Washington, D.C. or a fishing trip to Wyoming. Harden was not a story-teller or loud entertainer at his functions. Instead he commanded attention and respect when he walked into a room. His quiet presence made a difference. He did not waste words with busy talk but spoke only when he had something worthwhile to say. He had amazing charisma and a great sense of humor. He dominated the room.[221]

Harden was obsessed with keeping his hands perfectly manicured. It was as if he was trying to show everyone that he was not a manual laborer. It was not uncommon for him to have his nails manicured several times a week.[222]

Frances Harden poses with a grizzly bear she shot on a hunting expedition with her husband in Alaska in the 1930's. Courtesy John E. Harden.

Harden spared no expense in showing his friends a good time. He and his wife Frances entertained the prominent families of Oklahoma City in celebration of the major holidays, birthdays of the children, and for any other reason they could think of.

Seldom did Harden take only family members along on trips. He rubbed elbows with the rich and famous of America from the 1920's until his death. Through his friendship with Scripps-Howard chairman Roy Howard, Harden met and developed close relationships with three of America's leading writers and journalists.

Rex Beach was an American novelist with more than 30 books to his credit. He co-wrote the successful play *The Spoilers,* which was made into a movie. Beach was a "Jack London"-type character who enjoyed fishing and hunting with Harden and talking about gold mining. It was Beach's stories of gold mining in the Klondike in Alaska that whetted Harden's appetite for gold dust, an appetite that cost Harden substantial money in the 1930's and 1940's. Both Harden and Beach were born in Michigan.

Another frequent companion of Harden was Irving Shrewsbury Cobb, a Kentucky-born humorist and journalist who wrote for the *Saturday Evening Post* and *Cosmopolitan Magazine.* Cobb wrote 60 books including his most successful, *Old Judge Priest* in 1915.

Cobb's editor at *Cosmopolitan* was Ray Long who spent weeks at a time with Harden on fishing and hunting expeditions. Harden liked long visits with his friends. In December, 1931, he wrote

Rex Beach, "If it would be possible for you to come down for the month of December, we can have a lot of sport."[223]

Harden threw incredible parties in his suite at the Mayflower Hotel in Washington, D.C. when he was in the nation's capital on business. Attorney Phil Daugherty remembers seeing O.A. Cargill on a Washington street once. Cargill said, "Let's go to the Mayflower. Jack Harden is throwing a party."[224] Daugherty said the party was "too rough" and he had to leave after a few minutes. It was at one of the Washington parties that Harden met his second wife, Helen, secretary to U.S. Senator Huey P. Long.

Liquor flowed freely at Harden's gatherings. Liquor usually did not affect Harden's relationship with his guests, but the overdrinking was hard on the interaction with his family. On many occasions in his lifetime Harden spent weeks at a time "drying out" at spas in Texas, California, and New York.

Harden loved New York City. He usually made the Astor Hotel home base for his parties and receptions. Rex Beach, Irving Cobb, and Ray Long all lived and worked in New York City so Harden made it to the Big Apple as often as possible.

Harden had a variety of friends in New York City. Among his closest companions were Father J.F. Stillemans at St. Albert's Catholic Church on West 47th Street; Wall Street investment banker Herbert C. Heller; Joe Johnson, New York City's Public Works Commissioner and close associate of New York Governor and later presidential nominee Al Smith; and Will H. Hayes, president of the Motion Picture Producers of America.

Harden and Ponca City, Oklahoma oil millionaire Lew Wentz hosted a long-remembered private party in Philadelphia in September, 1926 on the night before boxing champion Gene Tunney outlasted Jack Dempsey for the heavyweight championship of the world. George Miller of the 101 Ranch in Oklahoma was one of Harden's famous Oklahoma guests at the party.

Also at the party was actress Billie Burke who is best remembered for her role as the Good Witch of the West in *The Wizard of Oz*. Burke was a wife of Flo Ziegfield of Ziegfield Follies.

THE SCRIPPS-HOWARD NEWSPAPERS

Sunday, October 30, 1927.

My dear John:

I got back to New York last night and going through my mail at home today found yours of October 17, also yours of the 20th and Macneish's letter of October 24. I have not seen Macneish yet but I take it that the betting matter is cleaned up. I'll have him get in touch with Heller early this week just to check up.

Had a very good time, though very poor shooting, up in the Canadian woods and came back full of pep and rarin' to go.

By this time you know of developments in the Oklahoma News office. Was sorry that I could not tell you in advance but it did not seem exactly fair to Evans to have anyone else know in advance of the time when Parker took things up with him relative to his stepping out of that particular picture. I guess you know something about Magee. I prefer to talk about the newspaper business in the past tense but I believe that without violating my usual conservatism I can assure you that from this time forward the Oklahoma News will have an entirely different editorial swing and punch than that which has characterized it recently.

I had a phone talk with Ray Long today and find that he has reservations out of New York for Cobb, Beach, himself and myself on November 16, which will put us into Tulsa on the morning of November 18. I'll appreciate it if you will drop me a line relative to weather conditions where we're going. I have duxback clothes with lined and unlined coats, sweaters, windbreakers, and so forth. I know that it is darned easy to be uncomfortable sitting in a boat on the water under dressed but at the same time I do not want to drag along a lot of unnecessary junk. I think I'll probably bring a duffel bag full of stuff and express it back home after I'm through with the shooting. Of course, I'll bring along my own shotgun.

Anything you can give me relative to details of the party, and so forth, will be appreciated.

Meantime, Peg and I are delighted to know that you and Frank are lending a responsive ear to the suggestion of a North African and European jaunt sometime the latter part of January or early in February.

We are going to have a big editorial conference about the middle of January and I feel that it will probably be impossible for me to get away much before the first of February. However, I think that is a pretty good time anyway, as it represents about the time that everybody is pretty well fed up with winter in this country.

If you have gotten any indications of how things are going, I'd be very much

Roy Howard and Harden constantly planned hunting and fishing expeditions.

Courtesy John E. Harden.

interested in having your opinion and ideas as to the action resulting from the announcement of Magee's move into Oklahoma City.

With kindest personal regards to Frank, the kids, and yourself, I am,

Faithfully yours,

John J. Harden, Esq.,
1711 Tradesmen Bldg.,
Oklahoma City, Okla.

RWH:AML

P.S

Cobb may not be able to stay as long as the rest of us but he is coming along anyway

ROY W. HOWARD
CHAIRMAN OF THE BOARD
250 PARK AVENUE
NEW YORK

September 29, 1928.

Dear John:

I was mighty happy to get your wire today saying that you were
on for the Wyoming shoot.

Here's the plan:

Those of us who are leaving New York will depart on the Century
October 12. We will be in Chicago at 9:40 A. M., Saturday
the 13th, and will leave Chicago Saturday at 12:12 (Noon)
the same day, via the Northern Pacific, for Billings,
Montana. We will arrive in Billings on the evening of the
14th at 11:31 P. M. and stay over night there and leave
at 7:30 on the morning of the 15th, via the Burlington,
for Cody, Wyoming -- arriving there at 12:30 (Noon). At
Cody we'll meet Ed Leech of the Denver News and the Wyoming
people who are to have charge of the party.

They will take us to the hunting lodge where we are to be housed
which is, I understand, about forty or forty-five miles outside of Cody. We'll be into camp and all fixed up on the
afternoon of the 16th.

According to present plans we will shoot on the 16th, 17th, 18th,
19th and 20th and, if in those five days we have sufficient
game, we will push off for home on the 21st. If we haven't
enough game we'll stay for a day or two longer until we get
enough.

I am going from Cody to Denver, stopping in Denver for a couple
of days and then return directly to New York.

The party will be limited to eight. Beside Ed Leech, myself and
yourself, there will be Karl Bickel, William G. Shephard,
associate editor of Collier's, Will Hays, probably Kent
Cooper of the Associated Press, and one other, probably
John Golden, the playwright and play producer.

Will Hays, who doesn't shoot, is going to take some motion picture paraphernalia and shoot movies instead of a gun.

In the meantime, with best regards and looking forward to a good
party, I am,

Faithfully yours,

John J. Harden, Esq.,
205 Petroleum Building,
Oklahoma City, Okla.
RWH:WEV
cc ETL KAB

Harden made an impression on Billie Burke. After she returned to her home at the 44 Street Hotel in New York City she wrote Harden suggesting that he look over her proposal for a touring water circus and a possible appearance by boxer Gene Tunney at the 101 Ranch in Oklahoma.[225]

Harden hunted quail and pheasant in the Salt Plains of Oklahoma and Nebraska, and sage hens in Wyoming. He meticulously planned and carried out deer and quail hunting and fishing trips to Old Mexico. He hunted bear in Alaska and big game in Africa.

Harden loved hunting in Oklahoma so much that he joined the Saline Game Preserve near Tulsa at the invitation of his accountant, F.C. Hays.

Harden took great pleasure in planning hunting and fishing trips down to the last detail. He sent specific instructions to guests. A typical letter read, "For the quail shooting a light leather boot, also a sleeveless skeleton hunting jacket. We will do our duck shooting from blinds. Don't believe we will have any trouble with the automatic but suggest you also bring your double barrel gun."[226]

One of Harden's most memorable hunts occurred in fall of 1927 when he, Rex Beach, Ray Long, Roy Howard, and Irving Cobb spent the night with George Miller at the 101 Ranch before hunting quail in nearby cornfields. Just before the hunt Harden had some repair work done for a painful hemorrhoid problem. He wrote Howard, "I've been in bed for days, having had a slight operation on my differential. I am feeling fine now. It looks like we're going to see plenty of birds."[227]

Years before he built a hotel in Acapulco, Harden spent vacations fishing the waters along the southern Mexican coast. Courtesy John E. Harden.

THE SCRIPPS-HOWARD NEWSPAPERS

Chicago, Ill.
September 7, 1927

Dear John:

The following is confidential and I will ask that you make no mention of
it but I think it will interest you:

The night before Peg and the kids left, as we were coming out of the dining
room of the Brown Palace, we encountered your friend Bonfils. Our
eyes met at identically the same instant. It is apparent to me that
he was hesitant as to whether to speak so I stepped in close and
greeted him. He responded very cordially and after I introduced
him to the family, with whom he chatted for a moment, then he turned
and whispered into my ear: "You and I are a couple of damn fools".

I replied that I knew one of us was but I did not know whether we could
make it unanimous. He then drew me to one side and began to explain
to me why he started the morning paper. I saw that he was anxious to
talk. So was I, but not briefly. If I talked at all I wanted to go
clear into the proposition. So as quickly as possible I got away
after having suggested to him that we get together, and asking him if
he would lunch with me. He said he'd be glad to.

Three days later at my invitation he came to my rooms at the hotel at
12.30 noon. We lunched and talked until 4.00 o'clock.

A lot of things developed that I will not take time to go into here. He
has his belly full of the morning paper. He's as tired (or moreso)
of losing a wad of money, as we are, and was entirely amenable to the
suggestion for eliminating a dozen wasteful practices in which we are
both engaging. The upshot of it was an agreement between him and me
to have his nephew and general manager, get together with our editor
and business manager with a view to cutting out this waste, and with
a view to each of us getting back onto our own side of the street
and playing our own game.

Of course, it remains to be seen what actually happens. I am sure no harm
was done. Considerable good may eventuate. I made a number of
suggestions to him as to how he might rid himself of the burden of
his morning paper without "losing face". I do not believe he will
avail himself of any one of these methods yet, but I think he will a
little later on. He's got to because he's hooked hopelessly --
truce or no truce -- so long as he holds on to his morning paper,
which he realizes is a dud and which he further realizes could not be
put over in five or ten years of effort.

I think that you broke the ice. I am very grateful and if we're able to
score a put-out, I'll give you credit for an assist.

I got a lot accomplished while in Denver and am immensely pleased with
     with improvement in our situation there. We've still a long fight
     ahead of us but we are getting a break and things are going to improve
     steadily but consistently.

My family left Denver several days ahead of me and are safely home now.

I am here fighting out a tangle in the matter of the fight broadcast and
     may be held here for a couple of days more. No serious difficulty
     but a kink that I want to get ironed out before I go on to New York.

Hope your family all got home okey. We regretted not seeing the important
     part of it again as they dashed through Denver but will hope for a
     reunion some time in the near future.

I don't expect to get immediate action but I've very definitely in mind the
     jazzing up of that Oklahoma situation as soon as Parker gets back to
     New York from Europe.

In the meantime I hope that you will give Pete Hamilton every opportunity
     to get acquainted with you. I am certain that he can get some advice
     and tips from you that will be of real value.

My regards to the family and the Ferguson's.

                              Faithfully yours,

John J. Harden, Esq.,
1711 Tradesmen Building,
Oklahoma City, Oklahoma.

P.S. Please tell Jane that I had to leave some of the films in Denver to
          get some prints made but I'll send them along to her a few days
          after my return to New York.
                              RWH

The "friend Bonfils" mentioned by Howard was the publisher of *The Denver Post*.
Courtesy John E. Harden.

ROY W. HOWARD
CHAIRMAN OF THE BOARD
250 PARK AVENUE
NEW YORK

Cosmopolitan Hotel,
Denver, Colorado,
November 8, 1928.

PERSONAL

My dear John:

Yours of October 31st has just reached me here. I am terribly sorry
to learn of John's accident but hope that the x-ray revealed no
serious complications.

With your worries over John's condition, I haven't had the heart to
ask you what became of those wires you were going to send me after
the election. In fact, I have been so busy working out the details
of this proposition here that I had not thought of your promise until Will Hays reminded me of it in a long distance talk I had with
him this morning on another matter. You made a great hit with
Hays and he wants to meet up with you again.

You will be interested to know that, as the result of developments here,
Bonfils and I, who seemed to have developed one of those friendships
that sometimes result from a good fight, are going to appear as
joint guests (don't misunderstand the use of that word, joint) at
a Chamber of Commerce luncheon, given to celebrate the peace, here
tomorrow.

If, by any chance, you should be dropping him a line congratulating him
on the sane settlement of this absurd situation, I wish you would
say that I told you -- what is a fact, namely -- that I never engaged in a negotiation with any man who was fairer or broader mind-
ed, once he was convinced of my sincerity, than was Bonfils. I
have a damned strong suspicion this man has the same capacity for
being an effective friend that he has for being an effective enemy.

This deal is going to net him an increase in profits of about a million
and a half a year and is going to convert a half million dollars a
year deficit, which we were enjoying, into an annual net profit of
somewhere between three hundred and five hundred thousand dollars.
Naturally, I felt that my "hunting expedition" was something of a
success.

Am leaving for French Lick Friday afternoon and expect to be back in New
York the last of next week.

Please extend my sympathy to John and my hopes for a speedy recovery.

Cordially yours,

John J. Harden, Esq.,
Suite 205,
Petroleum Building,
Oklahoma City, Okla.
RWH:WEV

                    February   1st,
                    1 9   2 9.

Roy W. Howard, Publisher,
New York Telegram,
New York, N. Y.

Dear Roy:-

          I just returned to Oklahoma City from
my hunt in Mexico, and certainly had a marvelous time,
with plenty of game of all kinds.   It is really a
marvelous spot for a hunt.   We had to do considerable
horse-back riding, but thank God, they were out of
mountains and snow down there.

          I am a little surprised to see you tying
yourself down to a real job, but I guess we all have
to do this once in a while.   You will remember that I
told you at the ranch that I was certainly going to get
out of a lot of my work, and I am in more things now
than at any other time in my life.   We finished a wonderful year with my ten small corporation, doing a gross
business of four millinn dollars.   This does'nt mean
much in New York, but it is a helluva business in this
country.

          I am not sure whether or not, I am going
to get to Palm Beach myself, because we have so many
things in the fire that I may have to stick on the job.

          With best wishes for a big year for the
Telegram, and I would certainly lay a little bet that
you put it over in big shape.

                              Yours sincerely,

JJH:H

In later years after Harden built his hotel in Acapulco, he was host to many famous Hollywood personalities. He hunted and fished and played cards with John Wayne who owned property near Acapulco. Harden described Wayne as "the finest young man I have ever met."[228]

Harden had a cabin cruiser anchored in Acapulco Bay. He used the boat for motoring along the beautiful coastline and for hosting gala parties with famous guests like Mexican President Miguel Aleman, former U.S. Ambassador to Mexico R.B. Creager, singer Frank Sinatra, actor Tyrone Power, and American Airlines president C.R. Smith.

When Harden stayed in California for any length of time he usually ended up drinking with actors Wallace Berry, W.C. Fields, and John Barrymore. Harden and his actor friends would often disappear on a "binge" for several days.

One of Harden's favorite spots on earth was his 33-acre Wyoming fishing paradise referred to as the "ranch." His daughter Jane had panned for gold on the property in the mid-1920's and had filed a claim on the picturesque valley for her father. It became the summer home of the Hardens for many years.

The ranch was located just east of the Continental Divide in the Medicine Bow mountain range of the Rocky Mountains in south central Wyoming. The property was on the Encampment River, just two miles from the town of the same name which was derived from tribes of Indians who annually gathered along the river in the nineteenth century in a "Grand Encampment."[229]

To permanently hold title to the land, Harden had to improve it within a short period of time. He contracted with the man who built the main lodge at Yellowstone National Park to construct a huge bunkhouse, called the Hardale Lodge, a combination of Harden and Hale, Frances Harden's maiden name, and two cabins out of logs from the forests of south-central Wyoming.

Harden had a timber and rock low-water dam built across the river, backing up water for miles to form a small lake about 12-feet deep. He installed a water wheel which generated electricity for the mini-resort. An ice house was built into the side of a mountain. In the winter, the resident caretaker, nicknamed "Slim," a full-blooded Indian, carved huge chunks of ice from the frozen river and stored them in the ice house for use in the summer.

The two cabins slept four to six people and were primarily used by guests. The resort could be used only in the summer because it was inaccessible for most of the harsh winter. The valley was located at 7,500 feet, making for cool nights even in the summer. Harden bragged, "You can sleep with the blankets over you every night, even in August."[230]

The main house was a large log building that comfortably slept 16 to 20 people. It had a large kitchen with a wood cook stove. The floors were covered with the skins of Kodiak bears shot by Harden in Alaska. Elephant tusks and the trophy heads of animals brought back from African safaris decorated the walls.

United States District Judge Edgar S. Vaught hunted and fished with Harden often at the ranch at Encampment. Courtesy Oklahoma Historical Society.

A separate bunkhouse was provided for maids and porters, who accompanied the family to Wyoming, and for a year-round caretaker.

For Harden the main benefit of the ranch for him was the availability of some of the world's finest fishing. Harden was a world-class fly fisherman. He bought bamboo rods from Scotland and frequented sporting goods stores such as Abercrombie and Fitch for his gear.

Harden liked to fish anywhere. But there was something special about the clear waters of Wyoming that soothed Harden's soul. He fished for German brown and rainbow trout on the Encampment and North Platte rivers. The Encampment emptied into the North Platte just a few miles east of the resort. Harden caught as many as 50 to 60 trout each day and told his friends that he could fish just by "stepping out of the house and walking up the Encampment River."231

Harden used the ranch for entertaining friends and political and business contacts. Many would spend just a few days of "good sport," as Harden called it. Others such as Rex Beach, Ray Long, Roy Howard, and U.S. District Judge Edgar Vaught of Oklahoma spent a month or more each summer fishing in the area.

Vaught spent much of the summer of 1948 at the ranch. He "hired" Harden's grandson David to retrieve fishing lures errantly deposited in the trees along the river. When Vaught prepared to leave, he paid David one dollar for each fly he had recovered all summer.

The visitors list at the ranch read like a Who's Who in America. In the early 1940's U.S. Senator, and later President Harry S. Truman fished and hunted with Harden. Joe Johnson and other top-level managers of Al Smith's presidential campaign in 1928 stayed at the resort which was a favorite fishing lodge for Jesse Jones, the Texas banker who was appointed by President Roosevelt as the Director of the Reconstruction Finance Corporation and later served as U.S. Secretary of Commerce. Roosevelt's campaign manager James Farley frequented the ranch, as did U.S. Senator Elmer Thomas and other members of the Oklahoma congressional delegation.

When an important government official such as Farley visited the Wyoming retreat, special arrangements had to be made for telephone access. The closest telephone was two miles away in the town of Encampment. One of Harden's porter's main duties was to drive the visiting official into Encampment every day to check with Washington to see how things were going.

One of Harden's most frequent guests at the ranch was John Coleman Pickett who made his home in nearby Cheyenne. Pickett was county attorney in Laramie County, Wyoming in the late 1920's and early 1930's and served from 1935 to 1949 as assistant U.S. Attorney for Wyoming. In 1949 he was appointed by President Truman to a judgeship on the U.S. Court of Appeals for the Tenth Circuit. Pickett became one of the most respected federal judges in America. He so loved the ranch property that he bought the resort from Harden's estate after Harden died. [232]

Guests hunted and fished in the day time and played games at night. There was plenty of whiskey to accompany games of bridge, canasta, poker and checkers. Games were basically the only night-time entertainment. Harden, and any family members staying at the ranch, always joined guests in the games.

Grandson David remembers sitting around at night in fan-backed chairs at a round leather table playing gin rummy with his grandfather. Harden never could get a good fit on his false teeth and spent much of his time "heating" the dentures in an effort to mold them to his mouth. He owned more than 30 sets of false teeth, in a lifelong search for a pair that would fit. Harden had lost his teeth early in life because he constantly sucked on rock candy that he carried in his pocket. He explained to friends that he was so poor as a child that he never could buy candy. He made up for it by always having a supply of candy, resulting in the demise of his natural teeth.

Harden kept a cigarette in his mouth much of the time. He squinted at his hand of cards as the smoke curled around his face, a sight that made a lasting impression on young David.[233]

Besides fishing, Encampment offered sage hen or prairie chicken hunting on a grand scale. In 1929 Harden invited several of his friends, including magazine editor Ray Long, for a major "chicken hunt."

Harden picked up the hunting party at the Union Pacific train station in nearby Rawlins. He had discovered "virgin territory where there are literally hundreds of sage chickens just waiting to be murdered."[234] In planning even the small details of the hunt, Harden wrote Long, "We will get at least 200 chickens in two days. We can carry ice enough to thoroughly freeze the birds so you can take them back to New York."[235]

                    June   15th.
                    1 9   2 9.

Mr. Roy Howard,
% Scripps-Howard Newspaper,
230 Park Avenue,
New York, N. Y.

Dear Roy:-

                I am planning to go to Encampment about
July 1st, and thinking further of the idea of meeting
you and Ray Long on your return from California, which
I think you said would be about August 4th, and here
is what I think would be a few days of real sport for
everybody.

                We could meet you at the Union Pacific
at Rawlins, Wyoming; this would probably be the same
train that you and Peg took when you left California,
and would arrive at Rawlins about 10 P. M. We would
go direct from there to the ranch, spending the night
there, get up about 6 A. M. the following morning and
be in the chicken shooting in about four hours.

                We discovered last year, virgin territory
where there are literally hundreds of sage chickens.
We did not discover this until after the hunting season
was closed, but the old territory that we would hunt
out on the way to the new field is good enough for anybody. Harry Cragin, Fred Clark and myself, and you
know what a wonderful shot I am, killed eighty-five
sage chickens in the old territory in about four hours.
This would only be a two-days hunt, because, I believe
we would get about two hundred chickens in this length
of time. We could take care of these in nice shape,
carrying enough ice to freeze them the same day that
they are killed. These could be kept frozen, and if
you and Ray wanted to take them to New York, it could
be arranged easily.   I have a further thought of
asking Fred Bonfils to join us on this two-day hunt.
After our hunt we could return to his camp and put in
two or three days fishing, or as much time as you and
Ray could spare.

#2.R.H:

        In the old days Bonfils used to have a
party of ten or twelve on these fishing expeditions
and they were mostly men of his age; since then a
great many of these fellows have died,and I imagine
that this whole program would suit him fine, because
we took him and a Doctor friend of his on the hunt
last year on an eleventh hour invitation. I have
not written him and will not until I hear from you,
but if this suits you, I will then get in touch with
Fred and we will have all arrangements made. We will
take our tenting equipment and camp on the banks of
the Little Savre river, and I believe you will have
the two best days of sport you have ever had in your
life, because as I told you in New York, even you,
Ray and myself can hit these chickens. I don't have
Gene this year, but really have a better nigger for
sporting expeditions; he will do our cooking and
take care of us in fine shape. Talk this over with
Ray and drop me a line as soon as you can, so that
I can make the proper arrangements. The only other
fellow who might be on this hunt is Harry Cragim,
although, Lew Wentz will probably be at the cottage
with the folks when you arrive, as you already know
he is not much on the hunting proposition.

        While in Florida, Rex Beach and Fred
Store took Frank and I to the fight,and I invited
them to be in Encampment the last of September, and
the first of August. This is quite indefinite, but
I am writing Rex and sending his letter in care of
Ray Long, as I have lost his address,and if they
should decide to stay until you and Ray arrive--that
much the better--because there are a million acres
to hunt over and not a house in the whole country.

        With best personal regards, I am,

                        Yours sincerely,

JJH:H

WAR WITH THE IRS

arden's free-wheeling attitude as a big-time gambler caused him to sometimes deal fast and loose with the Internal Revenue Service (IRS). He hired the best accountants, including R.M. Hays of Tulsa, and an internal auditor, C.J. Strong, to take advantage of legal loopholes or anything that reasonably appeared to Harden to be a loophole.

Even in years when he spent hundreds of thousands of dollars on vacations, gambling trips, and playing host to the rich and famous, his tax returns looked like those of a small business. 1928 was one of Harden's most successful years in business, yet his personal tax return reflected income of less than $30,000 with a tax liability of only $813.[236] His income came from so many corporations and partnerships, it was difficult to follow the money trail and determine his actual income and expenses.

Harden tried to write off as a tax-deduction almost any money he spent in pursuit of happiness or his business. Two deductions on his 1938 return for Harden Mortgage Loan Company landed him in hot water with the IRS.

Labeled as "road contract expense" was a deduction of $32,937.75, the amount paid by Harden Mortgage to one C.S. Beekman as commissions on sales of rock asphalt. The IRS disallowed the deduction as being against public policy. Facts gleaned from subsequent legal action in *Harden Mortgage Loan Company vs. the Commissioner of Internal Revenue*[237] paint an intriguing saga of alleged influence peddling at the highest levels of state government in Oklahoma.

The war with the IRS began when Harden Mortgage was notified June 30, 1941 that an additional $8,298.08 in federal income tax was due because the IRS disallowed the Beekman deduction and the attempted deduction of a $6,000 payment for "entertainment and traveling expense" made to New Mexico Congressman John J. Dempsey, a long-time associate of Harden. Similar deductions were disallowed by the IRS in 1936 and 1937. However, rather than pay the additional tax for 1938, Harden chose to fight the assessment. He later regretted that action.

Dempsey was a shareholder of the failed Continental Asphalt Company that operated the Dougherty asphalt mines. He later became president of U.S. Asphalt Company that bought the mines at a receiver's sale and leased them to Southern Rock Asphalt Company. Dempsey received royalty payments from Southern Rock Asphalt and even sold asphalt on commission to paving contractors in New Mexico.

For five years C.S. Beekman worked as an asphalt salesman for Southern Rock Asphalt Company and later for Harden Mortgage Loan Company when Southern Rock Asphalt was dissolved and became a division of Harden Mortgage. He had been in the asphalt business since shortly after statehood and was good at what he did. He was probably more of a lobbyist than he was a salesmen. His friends included members of the legislature, Highway Commission members, local and county government officials, and engineers of the State Highway Department who wrote specifications that governed what materials were used in road construction. Beekman did not work exclusively for Harden's enterprises. He also sold construction machinery and materials for several Oklahoma companies and claimed to have "sold more stuff than any man in Oklahoma."[238]

Beekman had a verbal contract with Harden to receive a ten percent commission on any sale of rock asphalt. Beekman sold more than $1 million of Harden's asphalt from 1933 to 1938, including sales of more than $200,000 in 1938, of which more than half were made directly to the Oklahoma Highway Department.

When Beekman became almost totally blind in early 1938 he formed a partnership to share in the commissions from the sale of rock asphalt. It was the notoriety of his partners that raised the hackles of the IRS.

The $32,000 commission in 1938 was paid by Harden Mortgage primarily to "Beekman and Company" and was split four ways among Beekman, Howard Drake, James C. Nance and Al G. Nichols.

Nichols was state senator from Wewoka, leader of the Democratic majority and chairman of the Roads Committee in the Oklahoma State Senate. He was often the author of Oklahoma's road construction laws that sailed through the legislature.

Howard Drake was a close friend of Governor E.W. Marland. He successfully managed Marland's campaign for governor in 1936.

The most famous member of Beekman's partnership was James C. "Jim" Nance of Purcell. Nance was one of the state's most powerful men, both in political and newspaper circles. He was born in 1893 in Arkansas and read law with his brother until "printer's ink" got in his blood and he determined in his heart to be a newspaperman.[239]

Nance owned a string of newspapers in Oklahoma and wrote editorials in his *Purcell Register* into his nineties. He was twice Speaker of the Oklahoma House of Representatives and also served as President Pro Tempore of the Oklahoma State Senate. He holds the rare distinction of presiding over both houses of Oklahoma's legislature.[240] In 1938 Nance was the majority leader of the State Senate.

Strong allegations of corruption were made by the IRS in a March 24, 1942 hearing in Tulsa before Charles P. Smith, a member of the U.S. Board of Tax Appeals. Harden Mortgage was represented in its appeal of the income tax assessment by Washington, D.C. tax lawyer George E.H. Goodner. The IRS was represented by its Assistant Division Counsel, James L. Backstrom, of Dallas.

In his opening salvo Backstrom accused Harden of making the payments to Beekman for the purpose of "influencing the Road Commission of the state of Oklahoma"[241] to award contracts to Harden or to other contractors who were forced to buy rock asphalt from Harden to meet strict specifications made by the State Highway Department. Backstrom argued that the payments should be disallowed as a legitimate income tax deduction because the payments were "clearly against public policy."[242]

Backstrom also labeled Harden's $6,000 payment to Congressman Dempsey as buying "influence."[243] Dempsey had strong ties to the Santa Fe Railroad and saved Harden large sums of money by convincing the Santa Fe to negotiate reasonable freight rates for moving rock asphalt from the mines at Dougherty to points in Oklahoma, Louisiana, and New Mexico.

Harden's attorney painted a picture of no wrongdoing, calling the payments to Beekman and Dempsey legitimate business expenses for services actually rendered Harden Mortgage. Roscoe Farmer, Harden's partner who had served stints as president and general manager of Southern Rock Asphalt before becoming vice-president of Harden Mortgage, testified that he had no knowledge of who Beekman's partners were in 1938.

Dempsey testified by affidavit that the $6,000 he received was for consultation "relating to freight rates, and expenses in connection with efforts to create a volume of material sales so as to reduce mining costs [for Southern Rock Asphalt], and many other sundry matters."[244] Dempsey stated he had made trips to Washington, Santa Fe, Chicago, and Oklahoma on behalf of Harden Mortgage and its asphalt strip-mining operation.

Beekman told the Tax Court that his office was a hotel room at the Huckins Hotel and that he hired Nance, Nichols, and Drake to "go out and work up propositions" for the sale of rock asphalt. He explained that competition for road building projects in Oklahoma was "very keen" and that sometimes he or his partners had to work on a project for two or three years before it came to fruition.[245]

Beekman denied that Nance or Nichols had anything to do

with the State Highway Department's adoption of regulations which often required the exclusive use of rock asphalt to pave state highways. However Beekman admitted that his partners regularly contacted members of the Oklahoma Highway Commission in efforts to promote the use of rock asphalt.

Beekman vehemently denied offering money to or actually paying any state official to recommend rock asphalt for a particular project.[246] He testified he saw Nance and Nichols hanging around the State Highway Department almost every day but saw no problem in the legislators helping him promote rock asphalt since the legislative session had ended for that year.

A subpoena was issued to Nance to testify at the March 24 hearing. However Nance did not testify and the official record does not reveal why he did not appear.

On July 27, 1942 the Tax Court issued a blistering opinion that upheld the IRS decision to disallow the payments to Beekman and Dempsey as deductions for Harden Mortgage Loan Company for 1938. The opinion concluded that the payment to Beekman was not intended solely for paying him for selling and promoting rock asphalt but had resulted in buying influence:

> Manifestly if a state highway were to be built requiring the use of rock asphalt for paving material the action of the legislature was necessary for the authorization of the highway and for the appropriation of money to build it. The influence of the political leaders of the majority party was necessary to effect this legislation. . . We do not think that it is material whether the petitioner paid the sums directly to these political leaders or to Beekman.[247]

The Tax Court ruled that the payment to Congressman Dempsey was not a legitimate ordinary and necessary expense of doing business and would be disallowed as a deduction.

Harden did not take the Tax Court decision lying down and ordered attorney Goodner to appeal the matter to the U.S. Court of Appeals for the Tenth Circuit in Denver. After hearing oral arguments in early 1943, the Tenth Circuit affirmed the Tax Court decision and ordered Harden Mortgage to pay the overdue tax that had ballooned to $15,000 with penalty and interest.

Harden was so angry that he hired Goodner to appeal the adverse decision to the U.S. Supreme Court. In the petition for a writ of certiorari Goodner alleged that the Circuit Court erred in holding Harden Mortgage guilty of practices contrary to public policy, "when petitioner merely contracted with Beekman, an independent contractor, to sell its product on a commission basis, even though it be held that Beekman and his associates did (unknown to petitioner) resort to practices contrary to pubic policy."[248]

Goodner argued that even if the Supreme Court held that the commissions paid to Beekman were for political influence, the payments should still be deductible in computing taxable income because "Congress has made no distinction between the taxable income of legal and illegal businesses."[249]

In November, 1943, the U.S. Supreme Court denied the petition for writ of certiorari, refusing to hear the case. The result was a final one. The decision of the U.S. Court of Appeals for the Tenth Circuit would stand as handed down. Harden Mortgage Loan Company had to pay, and pay they did.

BUSINESS AS USUAL

Harden was audited by the IRS almost every year from 1924 to 1945. But he successfully continued at the helm of his business empire as effects of the Great Depression waned in 1940 and America's intervention in the war in Europe became inevitable.

Harden's cemetery operations in Illinois, Texas, Ohio, and in Oklahoma City and Tulsa all were profitable. A new $250,000 mausoleum and crematory building was constructed at Memorial Park in Illinois in 1940 as the total value of that project rose to $2 million.

Cemetery lot sales at all of Harden's facilities were solid. When his mausoleums were full, he simply built more space, creating more opportunities for sales.

Harden was an Oklahoma delegate-at-large to the Democratic National Convention in Chicago in 1940, where there was talk of war.

As America's entry into the world war loomed on the horizon, Harden came up with a novel idea to stop Hitler if he should invade America. Recognizing that he had "never seen the National Guard drill" and that he knew "absolutely nothing about war," Harden wrote to Roy Howard about his idea, "If he [Hitler] should attack our eastern shores. . . Ford or General Motors should manufacture a hornet plane that would just be big enough to carry one pilot and machine gun to work on the enemy's infantry…The plane could be built for less than $10,000. They would not have much effect on tanks but would certainly raise Hell with infantry columns."[250]

Harden also proposed the construction of a small tank "which would operate the same as an automobile." He surmised that if the Army could hire the best automobile drivers in the country to drive the simple planes and tanks, the long nine-month pilot training programs could be eliminated. Harden admitted he had checked his plan with only one man, "a pilot in the last war in the French effort," the day before he wrote the letter to Howard.[251]

Harden's asphalt business boomed in the 1940's. Dump trucks and Harden's own railroad engine pulled railroad cars loaded with tons of rock asphalt from the strip mines near Dougherty to the Santa Fe siding for distribution to Oklahoma and New Mexico. By 1943 Harden's companies had mined 1.5 million tons of sand and gravel and 3.5 million tons of rock asphalt.[252]

Harden sold almost a half million dollars worth of rock asphalt annually until he exhausted the mines in Murray County. He landed large paving contracts all over Oklahoma including the contract for paving runways at Oklahoma City's new municipal airport. When the City Council approved Harden's airport paving bid over two lower bids, Mayor Frank Martin refused to sign the contract until forced to do so by court order. Martin, an attorney who had represented Harden over a decade before in Harden's successful attempt to build a farmers market, had become disenchanted with Harden and his business methods.[253]

During World War II Congress designated rock asphalt as a scarce natural resource and allowed producers a 15 percent depletion allowance. In theory the depletion allowance allowed producers of natural resources that were of a calculable finite amount to avoid some of the income taxes on profits as their resource deposit was being depleted. Similar depletion allowances had been enacted for oil producers during World War I.

In 1944 Congress revisited the issue of depletion allowances. Since rock asphalt was produced in only a half-dozen states, there was no hue and cry to retain the allowance after the end of the war. When the 1944 Revenue Act was written, rock asphalt was not included as one of the minerals that would retain the depletion allowance once the war emergency ended

House Resolution 7378 also proposed a tax of 90 percent on all income in excess of the depletion allowance. In other words the federal government would take, as an excess profits tax, 90 percent of profits that exceeded the taxpayer's average annual income for the previous four years.

The plan froze rock asphalt production at pre-war levels and discouraged companies from producing asphalt that was needed in large amounts for the war effort. To continue producing would mean not only no profit for Harden and other producers, but the loss of the reserves consumed in production as well.

Harden worked closely with Senator Elmer Thomas to assure the passage of an amendment that would give rock asphalt the same exemptions under the federal tax law as those given to oil and other depletable mineral resources. Harden joined with producers in Alabama, Kentucky, Texas, and California to hire Washington, D.C. lawyer George Goodner to carry their case to Congress.

In January, 1944, Thomas's amendment to the Revenue Act was defeated in the U.S. Senate by a slim margin, 38-34. However, Thomas was able to ultimately add rock asphalt to the list of minerals whose producers were exempt from excess profits tax for the remainder of World War II.

Harden continued to use his friendship with politicians and business leaders around the state to obtain paving contracts. The Lawton Chamber of Commerce had tried since 1936 to convince the federal government to provide monies through the WPA or the Civilian Conservation Corps for the hard surfacing of roads leading to Mt. Scott, a popular tourist destination near Lawton.

J.C. Kennedy, the 1939 chairman of the Good Roads Committee of the Lawton Chamber, joined forces with Harden who suggested that rock asphalt should be used to surface the Mt. Scott roads. Kennedy pleaded with Senator Elmer Thomas for help,

"The road up the mountain will undoubtedly wash badly and be dangerous to tourists unless it has hard surface at an early date."[254]

Harden, Thomas, and the Lawton Chamber of Commerce were successful in getting funds appropriated for the paving of the gullied roads leading to Mt. Scott. J.C. Kennedy later became one of Oklahoma's leading bankers and served on the Oklahoma Highway Commission and as State Democratic Chairman.

The oyster-shaped pool at the Hotel Palacio Tropical was the first hotel swimming pool in Acapulco. Courtesy John E. Harden.

HARDEN'S FOLLY

Why would a 61-year-old Oklahoma millionaire want to build a resort hotel in Acapulco, Mexico? Why not? That was the attitude of John J. Harden in 1945 when he bargained with Mexican officials for the right to build and operate an exclusive hotel in Acapulco, Mexico's oldest resort.

Acapulco was founded by the Spanish in 1550 and ultimately became the "Riviera of Mexico." During World War II many wealthy foreigners escaped war-torn Europe and landed in the resort famous for its excellent beaches and deep-sea fishing. Harden had visited Acapulco several times to fish the coastal waters and often thought of building a vacation home there.

In 1944 he found prices high and service poor at the few hotels in the city. Tourists were being gouged and Harden saw an excellent business opportunity for opening a first-class hotel with first-class service at a reasonable price. Harden thought the war would surely soon be over and tourists in America would be looking for low-cost vacations south of the border. Harden also was unhappy about his excess profits tax on U.S. earnings so he looked for projects for his companies to invest in.

Harden loved Acapulco, its bars, night spots, and the climate of the southern Pacific coast of Mexico. In his many visits to the area, he had become close friends with a very important Mexican citizen, Miguel Aleman Valdes, head of Mexico's tourism department.

Harden married his second wife, Helen (below, photographed with Harden at the Colonial House in Las Vegas), in Illinois in 1947. Courtesy *The Daily Oklahoman*. In Acapulco, the couple was photographed (bottom, below) with Jack Moreno in the restaurant at the Hotel Palacio Tropical. Harden hired Moreno to manage the hotel. Courtesy John E. Harden.

Aleman had previously served as governor of the Mexican state of Guerrero where Acapulco is located. He was interested in bringing American investment dollars to Mexico, especially to his home state. However Mexican laws in effect in 1945 made it nearly impossible for a foreigner to own property within 50 miles of the coastline. The policy was an attempt by a growing Mexico to keep its most valuable property and most lucrative business opportunities for its own citizens.

Aleman helped Harden get around the stringent Mexican rule by putting Harden in touch with lawyers in Mexico City to set up a Mexican corporation, Compania Comercial del Pacifico, S.A., as a legal front for Harden's interest in building a hotel. Harden Mortgage and Loan Company in Oklahoma City became the major stockholder of the Mexican corporation.

With a fist full of pesos and a strong will, Harden began construction of his hotel in the spring of 1945. Harden picked a spot of land on a hill overlooking Acapulco Bay and the Pacific Ocean. The view was incredible and so was the massive project of coordinating delivery of materials and hiring Mexican workers. Harden spent $2,000,000 to build his dream hotel.

Harden called his hotel the Casablanca. The hotel opened for business at Christmas in 1945. The Swiss architect who Harden had contracted with to build the hotel forgot a very important part of the project. There was no street up the hill to the hotel. The official opening of the hotel was delayed until crews built a makeshift road that afforded access to the hotel.

The Casablanca was the finest luxury resort hotel in Acapulco and had a well-deserved reputation as one of the best resort hotels in the world. Each of its 133 rooms and terraces had a view of "unsurpassed beauty."[255] Every room was air-conditioned and had a private bath, telephone, and terrace. A circular dining room and roof garden seated 500. A hotel brochure extolled the virtues of the Casablanca:

> The hotel is uniquely blessed with every advantage of location. Encompassed by views of both the ocean and the bay, the hotel looks down on the yacht harbor at its feet, daily aquaplane shows, the town itself, a diamond circlet of lights by night, and an ever-changing panorama of sea and sky and cloud-shadowed mountains by day.[256]

The four acres surrounding the hotel were covered with tropical vines and flowers and coconut palms, truly a paradise. Gift shops, a fully-equipped kitchen, and spacious gardens attracted thousands during the tourist season from mid-December to the end of March.

Harden tried to convince his youngest son Jimmy to move to Mexico and manage the hotel. Jimmy declined and Harden was left to find someone else to run the daily operations of the Casablanca. He met A.C. Blumenthal, "Blumy" to his friends. Blumy was a one-time Broadway producer who had moved to

Acapulco at the beginning of World War II and tried to buy the Hotel Reforma. Mexican officials balked at the deal and Blumy settled for the job of manager of Ciro's, Acapulco's hottest night spot located on the main floor of the Reforma.

Blumy leased the Casablanca from Harden and hired Teddy Stauffer, "Mr. Acapulco," to be the resident manager. Stauffer was a well-known German band leader before he emigrated to the United States at the beginning of World War II. When his visa expired he was stranded for nine months in the Mexican border town of Tijuana until he finally found paradise in the sleepy fishing village of Acapulco.

Stauffer, who became famous for his wives, including Hedy Lamarr, and his affairs with Rita Hayworth, and others, saved the Casablanca from bankruptcy in 1947 by building the Beachcomber Club, complete with an oyster-shaped swimming pool, the first pool at a hotel in Acapulco. Blumy vetoed the idea for a new and modern club in the hotel so Stauffer went directly to Harden. He traveled to Chicago and met Harden who gave Stauffer a tour of his mausoleum at nearby Evanston, Illinois.

Stauffer, in his autobiography, described Harden's Memorial Park Cemetery as "bigger than Acapulco, with lakes, hills and valleys; the largest and most scenic cemetery in the world."[257]

Harden stayed at the Casablanca for weeks at a time, entertaining dozens of guests, including his old friend Aleman who was elected President of Mexico in 1946. Until his death Harden maintained a personal suite in the hotel. Pained by family matters, according to Stauffer, Harden drank beer by the case, not purchased at his own hotel but at the Hotel Del Monte across from the Casablanca where beer cost 50 centavitos less per bottle.[258]

Stauffer was innovative in his efforts to revive the struggling hotel that locals called "Alcatraz" or "Harden's Folly." He hired divers to catch sea turtles in shallow water in Acapulco Bay or while they sunned themselves along the beach. The huge turtles were then transported to the Casablanca's large pool for "sea turtle racing." As strange as it seemed, large crowds of wealthy tourists were drawn to the daily races.

Palm trees lined the pool at the Hotel Palacio Tropical. Visitors were catered to by a staff of dozens of poolside waiters and assistants. The hotel commanded a spectacular view of Acapulco Bay. Courtesy John E. Harden.

Blumy fired Stauffer as resident manager of the hotel in 1948. In a few months employees of the hotel went on strike for back wages. After fifteen months of painful litigation, Harden forked over $200,000 and fired Blumy as manager of the hotel.[259] At first Blumy refused to leave the premises. Harden called upon President Aleman who promptly called out the Mexican National Guard to evict Blumy and his personal property from the hotel.

Harden was back at square one with a hotel that lost money or barely broke even most months. Over the next decade he hired a string of managers to keep the hotel alive. In addition to management problems Harden was threatened with a lawsuit over the use of the name Casablanca.

A veteran hotel manager Jack Moreno managed the hotel for several years. Harden's youngest daughter Frances blamed Moreno for the ultimate failure of the hotel. Frances accused Moreno of being planted in his position by another hotel owner who wanted Harden's hotel and that Moreno was "deliberately trying to depreciate the value of the hotel."[260] Frances felt Moreno began undermining Harden when it was discovered in April, 1961 that Harden had cancer. Frances alleged that Moreno began asking tour directors to pay bills in cash, forcing the directors to take their tourists to other hotels.[261]

The name of the hotel was eventually changed to Hotel Palacio Tropical. After John J. Harden died in 1962, his estate tried to operate the hotel until it could be sold. Jimmy Harden moved to Acapulco to manage the hotel. Unfortunately Jimmy liked to entertain large groups of friends who he allowed to stay free at the hotel.

The Harden Mortgage Loan Company, the hotel's majority owner, invested almost a half-million dollars in its renovation. In October, 1966, Jimmy was happy to report that the hotel had lost only 75,000 pesos, $6,000, for the year. Never did Jimmy report a profit on the hotel's operation.

In the end Harden's estate could not afford the outlay of tremendous sums of money needed to keep the hotel running. Large hotel chains built new resort hotels along the beach front and cost the Hotel Palacio Tropical needed business. Labor was an excessive cost because of the Mexican law that forced resort owners to hire employees year-round, not just in the tourist season. The estate eventually sold the once elegant resort hotel for $10,000 and relief from large loans that Jimmy Harden had obtained from Mexican banks to finance remodeling. Teddy Stauffer described the hotel in the 1970's as "merely a shell of a hotel, with occasional guests, mostly on package tours out of Mexico City, who are bused in via Cuernavaca and Taxco."[262]

The hotel in Acapulco was one of the few things in life touched by John J. Harden that did not turn to gold.

When the Hardens moved into their new home on N. W. 63rd Street in Oklahoma City, it was one of the finest and most modern homes in the state. The property included servants' quarters, an eight-car garage, and a working dairy. Courtesy John E. Harden.

THE FAMILY

John J. Harden possessed extraordinary skills that he used to develop solid relationships with friends, business partners, politicians, and customers. Sadly those skills never helped him in his relationship with members of his immediate family. By his death in 1962 Harden had somehow managed to alienate all his remaining family members.

Heavy drinking was a major problem in Harden's life. The drinking made him difficult to live with. Occasionally he made a

fool of himself even in public and to his friends. He once apologized to Ray Long, "I surely fell down on you the other night in New York, having been slightly over-trained from the previous evening."[263]

Harden never kicked the drinking habit. Time and again he dried out at spas. He once even went several months without drinking. In 1931 he wrote Roy Howard, "I do not know when I ever enjoyed a summer more, having been on the water wagon for about six months, I have found that you can really have some fun without a shot now and then."[264]

The Harden home was often filled with guests. Shortly after its completion, this lively group posed for a photographer. Frances "Lulie" Harden is at left. Roy Howard, in a bow tie, is flanked by his wife Peg on his right. To his left is Jane Harden. John J. is at the far right and young Jimmy Harden is in front. Courtesy John E. Harden.

Frances was active in several Oklahoma City women's and charitable organziations. She had spent the summer in Wyoming and the winter in California when the photos below were taken, and her return to Oklahoma City was news on the social pages of a local newspaper. Courtesy *The Daily Oklahoman.*

John J. and Frances Harden riding camels on a trip to Egypt in the 1920's. John J. is on the right. Frances, riding under the canopy on the middle camel, is wearing a white collar. Courtesy John E. Harden

John Hale Harden prepared his mount at the stable on the Harden estate on N. W. 63rd Street in Oklahoma City (shown at right). Courtesy John E. Harden.

Gambling was a passion. Harden bet on prize fights, political races and football and baseball games. He sometimes made money off gambling. He correctly picked Babe Ruth and the New York Yankees to win the World Series in October, 1927. However, when his bookie gave him a $5,000 hot check, Harden called on his high-placed friends Roy Howard and New York City Public Works Commissioner Joe Johnson to apply pressure on the firm that booked Harden's bets. Harden eventually received his money.

Harden gambled extensively in France in the 1920's and 1930's. He actually "broke the bank" at a casino in Deauxville, France in 1925. The French government would not allow Harden to take cash francs out of the country so Harden used his winnings, reported to the IRS on his 1925 return as $40,000, and bought diamonds and a Belgian-made Minerva automobile.

The cane-bodied Minerva town car was the Belgian Rolls Royce in 1925. The car was shipped from Antwerp, Belgium to New York City and then to Miami, Florida where Harden took possession and had it driven home to Oklahoma City. It sat in a Western Paving warehouse during the Depression because Harden felt badly about driving the luxury automobile around Oklahoma City. Eventually John Hale Harden sold the car to a junkman. Harden was not pleased when the new owner painted a sign on the car, "This car once owned by John J. Harden." Harden cringed when he saw the car being driven around the streets of Oklahoma City.[265]

Harden's successful businesses provided large amounts of cash for gambling in 1926 and 1927. In April, 1926 he gambled away more than $100,000 in French casinos. He purchased French francs from the Equitable Trust Company on Wall Street in New York City which transferred the money by wire to its bank in Paris. When Harden sailed to France, he drew down on his account and gambled for weeks.

In 1927 Harden lost another $123,700 gambling in France. Even though the IRS had required him to pay taxes on his winnings in 1925, the agency disallowed the huge loss in 1927 which Harden incurred at the Municipal Casino in Cannes in just 21 days. Records show that Harden wrote four checks to the casino for a total of $46,700 in just one day.[266] In current money values, Harden lost an equivalent of $986,000 in just three weeks.[267]

Harden hired a young Oklahoma City lawyer, Alfred P. Murrah, to sail to France to obtain necessary documentation to present to the IRS on Harden's gigantic gambling loss. In the end the IRS agreed with Harden's position, supported by information brought back by Murrah. The gambling loss was allowed as a deduction.

Back home Harden lost a sizable chunk of hard-earned money on the 1928 presidential election. He of course bet heavily on his candidate, Democrat Al Smith, who lost to Republican Herbert Hoover. Harden lost $6,000 to Lew Wentz of Ponca City and $3,000 each to John Phillips of Bartlesville and Bill Skelly of Tulsa.

When William G. "Bill" Skelly, president of Skelly Oil Company, acknowledged receipt of Harden's $3,000, he offered Harden advice, "If you want to offset your election losses, buy some Skelly Oil at the market and I am sure by Christmas you will make eight to ten dollars a share, with practically no danger of a loss."[268]

Harden's grandson, John E. Harden, nicknamed his grandmother, Frances Hale Harden, "Lulie," a name that stuck. John E. says Frances was the "class" in John J. Harden's life. Nicknames were prominent in the Harden family. Frances called her husband "Jack." He called her "Frank." They had worked closely together to build their fortune, until the 1920's when business was good and Frances no longer worked in the office.

In 1926 Frances picked the site for a new home, 2½ acres of land in Oklahoma City on N.W. 63rd Street between Grand Boulevard and Pennsylvania Avenue. She oversaw the construction of a large mansion, a two-story structure that contained almost 12,000 square feet.

The mansion had a full basement, a library containing 5,000 volumes, a living room with a concert grand piano, a solarium and an enormous dining room that could seat up to 50 people for dinner. Harden was always served first by a staff of eight servants, some of whom lived on the premises in adjacent servants' quarters in a separate building that also housed an eight-car garage.

Harden kept 10 to12 dairy cows to provide an adequate milk supply for a full-working dairy on the property at 1300 N.W. 63rd Street.

Frances was a marvelous party-giver. She socialized with the Nichols, the Buttrams, and the Johnsons. But she saved her most elaborate parties for special occasions such as birthdays and Easter. Her grandsons' birthday parties consisted of ice cream and cake, and were attended by dozens of neighborhood children. On George Washington's birthday Frances had ice cream concoctions made with little hatchets sticking out. At Easter 2,000 eggs were hidden on the grounds of the mansion.

Frances was also a first-class gambler. She gambled with her husband in France and was a frequent visitor to the Santa Anita race track in California. She was an International Grand Master duplicate at bridge and loved canasta, gin rummy, and any other game she could gamble on. Frances loved gambling about as much as her husband did. However Frances gambled and drank in moderation and could never understand how any one could be dominated by either.

Harden's alcohol abuse had a chilling effect upon his relationship with his wife. The marriage was troubled by the late 1920's and Harden had his lawyers draw up a separation agreement in 1930. The couple basically lived apart throughout the 1930's and 40's. Harden demanded a formal divorce in 1947.

Frances tried to keep the marriage together but could no longer overlook Harden's personality changes when he was drunk. A letter written by Frances to her husband in the summer of 1937 from Encampment revealed the terrible stresses placed on the marriage by alcohol:

You are right. We do love each other and the children all love you, but we couldn't go on the way we were, could we? Because nine-tenths of the time, you weren't yourself.

I know I would be terribly lonely to go on by myself, but I've been pretty lonely a lot of the time the last few years. Because there is no getting away from it, the old you, the one I loved and married, has not been much in evidence.

I know you've got a fight ahead of you. Jack, I can't very well meet you anywhere. The children need me. Jane is just verging on a nervous breakdown. Frances is a darling and grown very pretty but is about 30 pounds overweight. Jimmy, with his broken arm, needs my care.

I only want to do what is right and I would like to help you, only I never have known how, have I? If you want to come see the kids, I will go away while you're here. I wouldn't want us to get into any bitter controversies or any thing upsetting, because I am sure once you get your nerves in hand and definitely get away from liquor we would never have a word.

Jane and Jimmy and I have been saying a Rosary every night and maybe it will all work out. When Jimmy was hurt, and before I knew how bad, I thought maybe it was a judgment on us.

Well dear, we'll work it out, but let's go carefully and be sure and then we'll talk about starting new.

I love you and am standing by — Frank

Frances lived in Santa Barbara, California from the early 1940's until she moved back to Oklahoma City after Harden's death in 1962. Harden always provided financial support for Frances to live very comfortably, both before and after their divorce. Frances died in Oklahoma City in November, 1969.

The John J. Harden family experiment failed, despite a lavish lifestyle that provided unforgettable vacations and travels to all parts of the world. The Harden children could buy about anything they wanted, except peace and happiness.

HIS LAST YEARS

Harden spent his last years with his second wife, Helen Lynn Harden, whom he married in Evanston, Illinois November 30, 1947, shortly after he divorced Frances. Harden met Helen in the early 1930's when she worked for U.S. Senator Huey Long in Washington, D.C.

Harden moved Helen to Illinois in 1938 and made her his secretary at the Central Cemetery Company. She served as his mistress until the 1947 marriage. Harden's second try at marriage was as rocky as his first. In 1959 Helen sued Harden for divorce but dropped the idea as "soon as she knew what she was doing." She later blamed Jimmy Harden for causing problems between her and Harden, "He was my enemy, he tried to break up my marriage."[270]

Helen spoke Spanish fluently and became the business manager of Harden's Acapulco hotel in 1955 as she and Harden lived there much of the year.

In 1960 Harden's arthritis worsened and caused him great pain. In addition he was diagnosed with cancer. In a letter to son Jimmy, Harden said, "Some days I feel pretty good and then again there are days when I suffer great pain. We have fixed up an arrangement on the terrace where I can sit and get the benefit of the heat of the sun."[271]

Harden's condition did not deter him from hosting a gala party on the Starlight Roof of the hotel in 1960. Three hundred people, including actor Jack Lemmon and "movie stars galore—from England, South America, and Italy," drank and danced the night away until 5:00 a.m. Harden wrote, "They tell us that it was the best party of the entire festival so far. It will surely bring back the prestige of the hotel that we had before I got sick."[272]

Harden was overwhelmed by the stealing and cheating he found in the management of the Hotel Palacio Tropical. Of one manager he reported, "Main guy has been drinking and shooting at a guy while he brutally raped his wife."[273] Harden sent for his old bodyguard, Jelly Boyce in Oklahoma City. Harden recognized, at age 76, that he needed help. He wrote, "If I could turn back the pages of time eight years I wouldn't need any help."[274]

Harden became more difficult and cranky as old age and cancer crippled his body. He would ask Helen to come near him and then whack her with his cane. The last time David Harden saw his grandfather, Harden had fallen and broken a hip. David felt like he had an audience with a king who puffed on a cigarette and placed $50,000 bets on football games through his friend Wilbur Clark in Las Vegas.[275]

Harden died quietly in his sleep in Oklahoma City, August 29, 1962, a few weeks short of his 78th birthday.

Most of John J. Harden's life was embroiled in controversy. The probate of his estate was no different. Even before Harden was laid to rest the legal fight began. The day before his funeral attorneys for Helen filed a petition asking that a 1957 will that left basically everything to her be probated. Within days Frances hired attorney Phil Daugherty to contest the will.

Harden had executed a trust in 1942 leaving his estate to Frances, their children, his aunt and sister, and longtime business associates George Simpson and Roscoe D. Farmer. In the property settlement agreement in his 1947 divorce of Frances, Harden could not modify this trust agreement without the approval of Frances.

Daugherty filed a lawsuit on behalf of Frances against Helen, alleging that any will executed by Harden after 1947 without her consent was invalid.

Ironically, *Frances Hale Harden vs. Helen Lynn Harden* was assigned to Oklahoma County District Judge Clarence Mills, the legendary judge who had represented Harden before taking the bench and had allowed the adoption of John E. and David Harden over the objection of their natural mother.

The probate proceedings concerning Harden's two wills were heard by District Judge Harold Theus. Attorney Daugherty entered into a contingent fee contract with Frances. Daugherty was a veteran probate and trust attorney in Oklahoma City. He had practiced law since 1928 and was a partner with long-time attorney Fisher Ames.

On November 17, 1962, Judge Theus refused to admit either Harden will to probate, choosing instead to give priority to the terms of a trust Harden had created in 1947. Theus appointed two well-known Oklahoma City attorneys, William B. Rogers and John C. Andrews, as co-administrators of Harden's estate. Each were required to post $100,000 bond.

Rogers, Andrews, and Daugherty took over control of Harden's empire. Jimmy and Frances Harden lived in Oklahoma City and actively took part in making decisions affecting the John J. Harden Trust and its management of various business enterprises. Adopted sons John E. and David both lived out of the United States, making if difficult for them to have any input into the operation of the Harden Trust.

After three years of legal wrangling, a settlement of Harden's estate was reached in October, 1965. Helen Harden was awarded basically her widow's share allowed by law and one-third of the increase in value of Harden's businesses since their marriage in 1947. The remainder of the estate was split among first wife Frances; the two remaining Harden children, Jimmy and Frances; and the grandsons and adopted sons, John E. and David.

In 1998 John E. Harden was the only Harden heir who still owned any of John J. Harden's original property in Oklahoma City.

1. Alice Curtayne, *The Irish Story,* (New York: P.J. Kenedy and Sons, 1960), 342-43.
2. J.C. Beckett, *The Making of Modern Ireland,* (New York: Alfred A. Knopf, 1966), 339.
3. *Newman Grove Republic,* July 8, 1987, a reprint of an article that originally appeared in the newspaper in 1927.
4. Roy P. Stewart, *Born Grown,* (Oklahoma City: Fidelity Bank, 1974), 201.
5. Stewart, *Born Grown,* 162-163.
6. Contract between Ella Classen and James J. Harden, December 14, 1917.
7. *Ibid.*
8. Deed from Rose Hill Burial Park to John J. Harden, dated May 3, 1919, and filed May 20, 1919 in Book 211, Page 551 of the records of the Oklahoma County County Clerk.
9. Advertising brochure from the Harden files.
10. *Ibid.*
11. *Ibid.*
12. *Ibid.*
13. Creston Hills sales brochure from the Harden files.
14. *The Daily Oklahoman,* May 10, 1925.
15. *The Daily Oklahoman,* June 16, 1928.
16. *The Daily Oklahoman,* May 10, 1925.
17. *Ibid.*
18. *The Daily Oklahoman,* May 29, 1925.
19. *The Daily Oklahoman,* September 7, 1925.
20. *Ibid.*
21. Letter from Dalgleish to Harden, January 13, 1925.
22. Letter from Harden to country club members, January 13, 1925.
23. Letter from E.K. Gaylord to Harden, December 2, 1927.
24. From a promotional brochure found in the Harden files.
25. Good Roads, vol. 43, page 158, March 1, 1913.
26. Opal Hartsell Brown, Murray County, In the Heart of Eden (Wichita Falls, Texas: Nortex Press, 1977), 51-59.
27. From letters found in the files of Harden.
28. Interview with Phil Daugherty, February 20, 1997.
29. From tax returns and stock ledgers in the Harden files.
30. Letter from J.W. Teter to First National Bank, Amarillo, Texas, May 29, 1926.
31. From an advertising flyer in the Harden files.
32. *Amarillo Sunday News,* October 10, 1926.
33. *The Amarillo Globe,* October 5, 1926.
34. From an advertising brochure in the Harden files.
35. *Ibid.*
36. Letter from Harden to Lew Wentz, January 14, 1931.
37. Undated newspaper clipping from the Harden files.
38. Undated letter to Roy Howard from Harden.
39. *Santa Fe New Mexican,* October 28, 1927.
40. *Ibid.*
41. Information found in the archives of *The Daily Oklahoman,* on the back of a photo of Carl Magee.
42. The history of the *Oklahoma News* and other state newspapers appears in a wonderful book, *The Story of Oklahoma Newspapers, 1844 to 1984,* by L. Edward Carter,

published in 1985 in the Oklahoma Horizon Series by the Oklahoma Heritage Association.

43. Letter from A.R. Hubenstreet to Harden, November 23, 1927.

44. Letter from Harden to Magee, November 30, 1927.

45. From various clippings of Magee's columns found in the files of John J. Hardin.

46. *Oklahoma News,* June 23, 1928.

47. *Ibid.*

48. *Ibid.*

49. *Oklahoma News,* March 29, 1928.

50. Letter from Harden to Carl Magee, December 12, 1928.

51. *Ibid.*

52. *Ibid.*

53. *Oklahoma News,* March 29, 1928.

54. Letter from Harden to Roy Howard, January 14, 1928.

55. *Ibid.*

56. *Ibid.*

57. Telegram from Roy Howard to Harden, January 17, 1928.

58. Letter from Howard to Harden, May 7, 1928.

59. *Ibid.*

60. *Ibid.*

61. *Oklahoma News,* June 21, 1928.

62. Letter from Howard to Harden, November 28, 1928.

63. *The Daily Oklahoman,* July 12, 1928.

64. *Ibid.*

65. *Ibid.*

66. *Ibid.*

67. *Oklahoma News,* July 13, 1928.

68. *Oklahoma News,* July 19, 1928.

69. Letter from Charles Henson to Harden, July 13, 1928.

70. *Tulsa Daily World,* November 10, 1929.

71. *Ibid.*

72. *Oklahoma News,* July 28, 1928.

73. *Oklahoma News,* July 18, 1928.

74. Letter from Howard to Roy Howard, October 20, 1933.

75. Letter from Roy Howard to Harden, October 31, 1933.

76. *The Outlook,* a magazine published in New York City, November 14, 1923, found in the archives of the Oklahoma Department of Libraries.

77. Charles Alexander, *The Ku Klux Klan in the Southwest,* (Norman: University of Oklahoma Press, 1995), 60.

78. *Madill Record,* September 13, 1923.

79. Richard O'Connor, *The First Hurrah,* (New York: G.P. Putnam's Sons, 1970), 33.

80. Letter from Joe Johnson to Harden, July 26, 1926.

81. Letter from Harden to Joe Johnson, July 19, 1926.

82. O.A. Cargill, *My First 80 Years,* (Oklahoma City: Banner Book Co., 1965), 178.

83. Letter from Harden to Joe Johnson, July 19, 1926.

84. *Ibid.*

85. *Ibid.*

86. Letter from Harden to Joe Johnson, February 4, 1928.

87. *Ibid.*

88. Letter from Harden to Joe Johnson, February 28, 1928.

89. *Ibid.*

90. Letter from Harden to Governor Al Smith, March 10, 1928.

91. Letter from Harden to Joe Johnson, April 11, 1928.

92. Letter from Harden to James J. Walker, May 3, 1928.

93. *Ibid.*

94. *Tulsa Tribune,* May 13, 1928.

95. *Oklahoma News,* June 28, 1928.

96. Alfred E. Smith, *Up to Now,* (New York: The Viking Press, 1929), 288.

97. *The Daily Oklahoman,* June 28, 1928.

98. Letter from Harden to George Van Namee, July 2, 1926.

99. Letter from Harden to George Van
Namee, July 5, 1928.
100. Letter from Joe Johnson to Harden,
August 1, 1928.
101. *The Daily Oklahoman,* September
21, 1928.
102. *Ibid.*
103. *Ibid.*
104. Smith, *Up To Now,* 397.
105. Matthew and Hannah Josephson, *Al
Smith: Hero of the Cities,* (Boston,
Houghton Mifflin Company,
1969), 385.
106. *Ibid.*
107. Smith, *Up to Now,* page 397.
108. Letter from Harden to mayor and
City Council, June 28, 1927.
109. *Oklahoma News,* August 27.
110. *Oklahoma News,* August 26, 1927.
111. *Oklahoma City Times,* August 30,
1927.
112. *Oklahoma News,* September 2, 1997.
113. *The Daily Oklahoman,* June 16,
1928.
114. *Ibid.*
115. *Oklahoma City Times,* June 16, 1928.
116. *Sunday Oklahoman,* June 17, 1928.
117. *Oklahoma News,* June 20, 1928.
118. *Ibid.*
119. Bob Burke and Von Russell Creel,
Lyle Boren: Rebel Congressman,
(Oklahoma City: Western Heritage
Books, 1988), 30-32.
120. Stewart, *Born Grown,* 234.
121. From financial statements of other
accounting documents in the
Harden files.
122. *Ibid.*
123. *Ibid.*
124. *Ibid.*
125. *The Daily Oklahoman,* February 9,
1930.
126. Stewart, *Born Grown,* 235.
127. *Ibid.,* 236.
128. From monthly financial statements
in the Harden files.
129. Letter from Harden to Vernon C.

Hastings, December 1, 1930.
130. Letter from Harden to Roy Howard,
March 19, 1932.
131. Letter from Harden to Rex Beach,
March 16, 1932.
132. *Ibid.*
133. Letters from Harden to John Hale
Harden at Battle Mountain, 1933.
134. Letter from John Hale Harden to
John J. Harden, July 22, 1933.
135. *Ibid.*
136. Letter from Harden to John Hale
Harden, September 8, 1933.
137. Letter from John Hale Harden to
Harden, November 13, 1933.
138. *Ibid.*
139. *The Daily Oklahoman,* November 1,
1930.
140. *Ibid.,* November 6, 1930.
141. *Ibid.*
142. *Oklahoma City Times,* November 6,
1930.
143. *Ibid.*
144. *Ibid.*
145. *Oklahoma News,* November 6, 1930.
146. *Oklahoma City Times,* November 12,
1930.
147. *Oklahoma News,* November 12,
1930.
148. *Oklahoma News,* November 20,
1930.
149. Letter from Harden to Jesse H.
Jones, December 13, 1930.
150. *The Daily Oklahoman,* October 25,
1931.
151. *The Daily Oklahoman,* October 27,
1931.
152. *The Daily Oklahoman,* October 28,
1931.
153. Discovery Claim, June 20, 1936.
154. *Oklahoma City Times,* Novmeber 10,
1930.
155. *The Daily Oklahoman,* Novmeber
11, 1930.
156. *Oklahoma City Times,* November 19,
1930.
157. Letter from Elmer Thomas to

Harden, January 16, 1933.

158. Telegram from Thomas to Harden, November 2, 1933.

159. Letter from Harden to Thomas, April 10, 1933.

160. *Ibid.*

161. Letter from Harden to Thomas, September 20, 1933.

162. Ibid.

163. Telegram from Davis Chamber of Commerce to Senator Elmer Thomas, October 26, 1933.

164. Telegram from Harden to Senator Elmer Thomas, November 3, 1933.

165. Letter from Harden to Senator Elmer Thomas, December 26, 1933.

166. Telegram from a committee of miners to President Roosevelt, October 29, 1935.

167. Letter from Thomas to H.M. Arnold, Septmeber 22, 1935.

168. Letter from Harden to Scott Ferris, April 1, 1936.

169. Letter from Harden to Governor E.W. Marland, April 2, 1935.

170. Letter from Harden to RFC, September 18, 1935.

171. *Ibid.*

172. Letter from Harden to John Hale Harden, April 10, 1936.

173. *Ibid.*

174. Letter from Harden to Walter Harrison, January 15, 1936.

175. *Ibid.*

176. *Tulsa Daily World,* May 21, 1937.

177. *Oklahoma News,* July 21, 1938.

178. *Ibid.*

179. *Ibid.*

180. *Oklahoma News,* August 9, 1938.

181. *Oklahoma News,* July 31, 1938.

182. *Oklahoma News,* October 16, 1929.

183. *Ibid.*

184. *Oklahoma News,* Ocotber 19, 1929.

185. *Ibid.*

186. *Oklahoma News,* October 21, 1929.

187. *Ibid.*

188. *Oklahoma News,* October 5, 1929.

189. *Oklahoma News,* November 19, 1931.

190. *Ibid.*

191. *Oklahoma City Times,* March 18, 1931.

192. *Ibid.*

193. Stewart, *Born Grown,* 126.

194. Letter from Eulah Herr to Harden, February 26, 1930.

195. Letter from Farley to Harden, June 26, 1931.

196. Letter from Harden to Howard, June 15, 1932.

197. *Ibid.*

198. Letter from Harden to Howard, July 13, 1932.

199. *Ibid.*

200. Letter from Harden to F.B. Swank, April 26, 1934.

201. Letter from Harden to Joseph Johnson, October 22, 1936.

202. Telegram from Harden to President Roosevelt, November 4, 1936.

203. Telegram from Morgan to Harden, November 19, 1936.

204. Letter from Cartwright to Harden, January 5, 1940.

205. Telegram from Harden to Forbes Morgan, Secretary of the DNC, May 8, 1936.

206. Telegram from Harden to Congressman Nichols, February 6, 1936.

207. Telegram from Harden to Charles Mandeville of the RFC, June 10, 1935.

208. *Ibid.*

209. Letters from Elmer Thomas to Harden, March 25, 1936 and from Stewart McDonald to Elmer Thomas, March 22, 1938.

210. Letter from Harden to Thomas, January 27, 1937.

211. Letter from Harden to Thomas, December 13, 1938.

212. Telegram from Harden to the Mayflower Market, December 23, 1937.

213. Letter from Harden to Harry Hopkins, July 13, 1938.

214. *Ibid.*

215. *Ibid.*

216. Letter from Farley to Harden, June 8, 1937.

217. Letter from Harden to Farley, June 21, 1937.

218. The detailed story of Murrah's nomination as federal judge is found in *An American Jurist, The Life of Alfred P. Murrah,* by Von Russell Creel, Bob Burke, and Kenny Franks, (Oklahoma City: Western Heritage Books, 1996), 44-61.

219. Creel, *An American Jurist,* 55.

220. Telegram from Murrah to Harden, February 8, 1937.

221. Interview with David Harden, March 1, 1997.

222. *Ibid.*

223. Letter from Harden to Rex Beach, December 5, 1931.

224. Interview with Phil Daugherty, February 15, 1997.

225. Letter from Billie Burke to Harden, October 7, 1926.

226. Letter from Harden to Rex Beach, November 8, 1927.

227. Letter from Harden to Rex Beach, October 14, 1927.

228. Interview with David Harden, March 1, 1997.

229. The descriptions of the ranch come from interviews with Harden's grandsons, John E. and David Harden, who spent entire summers at the lodge.

230. Letter from Harden to James Farley, June 21,1937.

231. Letter from Harden to Rex Beach, July 19, 1926.

232. Creel, An American Jurist, 137.

233. Personal descriptions of Harden are derived from his extensive correspondence and from interviews with John E. and David Harden.

234. Letter from Harden to Roy Howard, June 15, 1929.

235. Letter from Harden to Ray Long, June 15, 1929.

236. Information from a review of Harden's personal tax returns and the returns of his many enterprises.

237. The opinion of the United States Board of Tax appeals was not formally reported. The 1943 opinion of the U.S. Circuit of Appeals for the Tenth Circuit is reported at 137 F. 2d 282.

238. Transcript of proceedings before the U.S. Circuit Court of Appeals, page 49.

239. The interesting story of Jim Nance is found in *The Story of Oklahoma Newspapers 1844 to 1984* by L. Edward Carter, (Oklahoma City: Western Heritage Books, 1984). Please consult the index for the many references to Nance.

240. *Ibid.*

241. Transcript of U.S. Board of Tax Appeals hearing, March 24, 1942, docket No. 108,731, page 14.

242. *Ibid.*

243. *Ibid.,* page 15.

244. Affidavit of John J. Dempsey, April 1, 1941.

245. U.S. Board of Tax Appeals transcript, page 97.

246. *Ibid.,* page 102.

247. Opinion by Charles P. Smith, member of the U.S. Board of Tax Appeals, July 27, 1942.

248. Petition for a writ of certiorari to the U.S. Circuit Court of Appeals for the Tenth Circuit, in the Supreme Court of the United States, No. 443, October, 1943, page 5.

249. *Ibid.*, page 7.
250. Letter from Harden to Roy Howard, June 15, 1940.
251. *Ibid.*
252. Brown, *Murray County History,* page 60.
253. *Oklahoma News,* August 23, 1938.
254. Letter from Kennedy to Thomas, January 6, 1939.
255. Hotel brochure in the files of John J. Harden.
256. *Ibid.*
257. Teddy Stauffer, *Forever Is a Hell of a Long Time,* (Chicago, Henry Regnery Company, 1976), 245.
258. *Ibid.*
259. *Ibid.*
260. *Ibid.,* 270.
261. Letter from Frances Harden in the files of John J. Harden.
262. *Ibid.*
263. Stauffer, *Forever Is a Hell of a Long Time,* 270.
264. Letter from Harden to Ray Long, June 15, 1929.
265. Letter from Harden to Roy Howard, November 4, 1931.
266. Interview with David Harden, March 1, 1997.
267. Letter from Harden to the Municipal Casino in Cannes, France, April 12, 1928.
268. The consumer price index published by the U.S. Department of Labor.
269. Letter from W.G. Skelly to Harden, November 17, 1928.
270. Inteview with John E. Harden, February 15, 1997.
271. The history of the relationship between John J. and Helen Harden is told in her own words in a September 18, 1962 deposition taken in the battle over Harden's estate, Frances Hale Harden vs. Helen Lynn Harden, No. 157-683, District Court of Oklahoma County, Oklahoma.
272. Letter from Harden to Jimmy Harden, November 30, 1960.
273. *Ibid.*
274. *Ibid.*
275. Undated letter from Harden to Jimmy Harden, in 1960.
276. Interview with David Harden, March 1, 1997.